Positive Attraction

Positive Attraction

Seven Simple Steps for More Love, Money, and Happiness

Walter Marin

Gomari Group
Austin

Copyright © 2014 by
Walter Marin

All rights reserved. No part of this book may be used or reproduced in any manner without the express written consent of the publisher, except in the case of brief excerpts in critical reviews or articles.

The content and advice in this book are not intended to substitute for the advice of a qualified physician or other licensed health care professional. All the information in this book is for educational purposes only.

Similar subjects include self help books, self improvement, the secret law of attraction, love, wealth, improving relationships, making money, health, and happiness.

Positive Attraction, Positive Attraction System, The Positive Attraction System, and Positive Attraction Academy are trademarks and/or service marks of Walter Marin in the United States and other countries. They are covered by appropriate domestic and/or foreign registrations and/or protective laws.

First Edition

Library of Congress Control Number: 2014933518

ISBN: 978-0-9910639-0-1
ISBN: 978-0-9910639-2-5 (ebook)

We hope you enjoy this book from Gomari Group. For book purchases, please e-mail our Special Markets Department: booksales@gomari.com

Published in the United States by
Gomari Group, Inc
Austin, Texas

To my mother, Linda, and brother Ivan for the great amount of love, support, and laughter they've shared with me throughout the years.

Contents

	Preface	11
	Introduction	21
1.	Prepare Yourself to Attract All That Is Best for You	25
2.	Step #1: What Do You Really Want? Define Your Desire	37
3.	Step #2: Think—It's All in Your Head	49
4.	Step #3: Take Action!	75
5.	Step #4: Feel—Happiness Is the Key to Success	125
6.	Step #5: Visualize—Imagine It in Your Mind to Have It in Your Hand	165
7.	Step #6: Have Faith—What I Truly Believe I Will Achieve	181
8.	Step #7: Receive Your Desire with Open Arms	193
9.	Results Are Always in Your Best Interest	197
10.	A Personal Word	207

Preface

Growing up in a middle-class family in San Diego, I was surrounded by loving people and blessed with everything a boy could ever want. After a few years of happiness, though, the blinders came off, and I began to notice the many issues my parents were going through in their marriage.

My parents tried to keep their conflicts hidden from my brother and me, but after some time, the arguments started to worsen. Some nights I could hear them screaming at each other and my mother crying.

Since my father worked many miles away, he would leave early and come home late. We rarely saw him, and this created emotional high and lows for all of us, depending on when he was home.

The whole problematic situation came to an end when I was about ten years old.

I clearly remember my mother telling me the news: they were getting a divorce.

My eyes filled with tears. Shocked, I ran outside, got on my bicycle, and rode it as fast as I could into the hills. I thought that if I pedaled hard enough, my speed would leave the pain and sorrow behind me.

After my parents' divorce, my brother Ivan and I lived in different parts of San Diego, mostly with our mother, a few years with our father, and even a year with our grandparents. This, of course, meant that I ended up going to many different schools. All these changes molded me into a very flexible and adaptive person. Throughout my childhood I learned a great deal and kept the positive attitude I naturally had. I always extracted the good from any bad situation that arose.

As I grew up, my circumstances kept improving for me. The older I grew, the more I was able to mold my life into whatever I desired and benefited me the most. Although I wasn't aware of it, I was naturally implementing the Positive Attraction System in my life.

What I Believed, I Achieved

Throughout my life, I believed that I could achieve whatever I wanted to, so I did:

- I loved the ocean and wanted to go scuba diving, and by the age of sixteen, I'd become a certified open water diver.
- I wanted to go to Europe and travel the world. My uncle frequently traveled, so I began to accompany him on his trips. By the age of eighteen, I'd traveled to over twenty countries.
- I really liked business in addition to travel, so I obtained a bachelor's degree in international business and, while I was at it, a personal financial planning certificate as well.
- I later wanted a master's degree in something more challenging like finance, so I obtained that as well.
- When I heard about a casting call for what at the time was an unknown movie called Titanic with Leonardo DiCaprio, I gave that a shot. I ended up being a featured extra and also worked on production for about half a year. I enjoyed that experience, so I later worked in production on a movie with Robert Downey Jr. and Annette Bening.
- I didn't want to spend a lifetime working for someone else, so I decided to become an entrepreneur and create my own business. I wanted a company that would generate lots of money yet still give me plenty of free time to do what I wanted. By the age of twenty-eight, I'd built an online travel business with over a million dollars in yearly sales.
- I liked martial arts and wanted to obtain a black belt, so I joined a Tae Kwon Do class and in a few short years earned my black belt. I liked it so much that I kept practicing and later received my second-degree black belt.
- And so on...

Everything was going great in my life up until my late twenties, when it all abruptly took a turn for the worse. I found myself in a very negative situation, one that would force me to analyze my life in an attempt to discover what it was that had previously made me so successful at obtaining all that I wanted.

The Eye-Opening Process Begins

In 2001, the whole world was altered by a major event that took place in New York City. My life, like that of many others, was sidetracked. In the span of one day, my online travel business went from being very lucrative to having almost no income at all.

After the initial shock of what had happened and the negative effects it produced in my life, a huge amount of emotional pressure started to build up inside of me.

Everywhere I looked and everything I did seemed to yield negative results.

My mind was filled with negative thoughts. I became so overwhelmed by them that when my girlfriend at the time told me she was going to go study abroad for a few months, I abruptly ended the relationship. I later regretted my decision, but it was too late: she decided not to come back, and my heart was broken.

Everything in my life was collapsing around me. My office, even though it was full of employees, came to a standstill because the lack of customers. Very few sales came in, and the money that had been saved was quickly being depleted. Soon there was only enough money to pay for rent and employees, and no matter what I did, I eventually had to close the business.

A few months later, my grandfather, who was my hero and mentor, developed health issues and passed away.

My emotions were in the gutter. Everything had come together, one negative event after another, to create the perfect mental, physical, and emotional storm.

I began to eat unhealthy food, I stopped going to the gym, and soon I started to believe that there was no way out.

As time went by, my lifestyle became more stagnant, and I remained in my apartment for longer periods of time. I socialized less, and, for the first time in my life, I was becoming overweight. The more I looked in the mirror, the less I recognized myself.

I also owed many months of back rent and car payments, and my debts kept increasing. It seemed as if new past-due bills came in every week while the emptiness and pain inside me kept growing.

The little money that came in went for food and to whatever creditor bothered me the most, in an attempt to lessen the amount of stress and pain that enveloped my life.

In a matter of months, I'd gone from having a life full of positive energy, people, and events to the complete opposite. What had taken me years to achieve and build up was quickly destroyed.

This situation was new to me, and I realized I was experiencing an emotion that I had never felt before: helplessness.

It all hit me with such speed that I didn't know how to react. I had always been able to stand up quickly whenever I had fallen, but this time was different. This time, no matter what I did, my situation kept worsening.

The combination of being emotionally drained, physically deteriorated, and financially wiped out was overwhelming.

It felt as if I had been thrown into an ice-cold river during wintertime, a river in the middle of nowhere, flowing with freezing water. And no matter what I did, I was unable to get out.

I had come to the point where I needed assistance from friends and family. I was so blind to reality that the only possible solution I could see was to borrow money in order to relieve, at least temporarily, the pressures and problems that surrounded me.

This later proved to be a guaranteed method of bringing more financial problems my way. Borrowing and creating new debts to pay off old ones began to convert friends and family into creditors. Instead of asking how I was and offering support in my time of need, they were asking when they were going to get their money back. I'd resorted to a short-term solution with possible long-term consequences.

I even rewrote the famous saying about money and applied it to my experience: "Money may not buy happiness, but the lack of money can guarantee you problems."

In truth, the world had not shut its door on me, but I *thought* that it had. The bad decisions I'd made, along with their negative effects, led to the negative thoughts that caused me to stop taking the necessary actions to improve my life. And the less I did, the more my problems increased.

PREFACE

Problems came at the most inopportune times and seemed to be poking me in my ribs to distract me, though I was trying my best to concentrate on improving my situation and bettering myself. Whenever it seemed that I had a good idea, whenever there was a glimmer of hope and I seemed to be gaining some momentum, something always caused me to lose focus and redirect my attention. Whenever I was rising up, an issue came that pushed me back down.

Constant distractions stood up as walls, preventing me from focusing on what really mattered and guaranteeing that I stayed down-and-out. I was forced to pay attention to my exterior and material circumstances while leaving my interior unattended.

After more than two years of the situation constantly worsening, I decided I needed outside help. My family and friends had always been supportive, but the type of support I needed was neither emotional nor financial; I needed to be shown the way to self-empowerment. I needed someone to lift my spirits and bring me back to being the positive and energetic person I knew I still was.

When I was sixteen, an uncle of mine bought a self-improvement system by a famous coach who sold his products through packaged books, audio recordings, and videos. Although I thought it was a great idea, at that young age, my mind was on other things. But the seed had been planted, and many years later when this negative situation arose, I remembered that self-improvement system.

I was determined to get out of my current situation and improve my life. I had defined my goal, so I took action and was able to get the tools and materials I needed.

After weeks of learning and trying to motivate myself, I got fed up with my situation. I clearly remember that I was lying in bed at two in the afternoon (yes, in broad daylight), wishing that all the problems and negative situations in my life would just magically disappear.

Then, suddenly, I had an idea, one that would help stop all the noise created by the problematic circumstances that were constantly distracting me and keeping me from seeing the light. It was one of the many ways I would come to discover of how to analyze and improve my situations more effectively.

I imagined seeing myself from the outside, as if I were floating a few feet from my body and looking down on myself. I was looking at my surroundings, the situations I had gotten myself into, and my life as a whole, but I was seeing them from the perspective of someone neutral and unbiased, someone caring and open-minded who would analyze my situation for the first time.

Seeing myself this way helped me assess the situation and gave me ideas about what I needed to do.

When you stop the noise and quiet your mind, powerful ideas come to the surface.

I had always been a positive person before, so why couldn't I continue down that same road? What had changed? When I analyzed my life, the causes of the situations, and the effects they'd brought upon me, I noticed a domino effect: my negative thoughts and actions had triggered other negative events and brought a life full of negative reactions. Suddenly the solution seemed simple. If I continued to do nothing, the negative situations would worsen and have control over me. If I took action, I would regain control.

I knew that what I had been doing for the last couple of years didn't work, so I simply decided to do the opposite. Doing something—anything—to try to improve my situation was better than doing nothing and continuing to spiral downward.

If normally I would get on my computer for a short while and then go back to bed (regardless of what time it was), now the first thing I would do was get the heck out of bed and keep moving. I started to work out again and take care of my body. I really enjoyed running; it cleared my mind, and it's one of the few exercises that requires only a pair of tennis shoes.

I got in touch with friends and family that I had slowly but surely pushed aside during this negative episode. Contacting them brought good memories and reaffirmed that I was still loved and appreciated. This started to fill me with positive feelings and energies.

I began to notice that during all the time that had passed, I had been blind. Once I understood that I had the power to choose what to bring into my life, I was able to change my outlook. All of us have this power. When you change and improve the way you think and follow through with action, your external world starts to follow and improve along with you.

For too long I had my doors closed to any and all opportunities, thinking they were useless and couldn't help me in any way. Since those incorrect decisions were a major part of the reason I was in this negative situation, I decided to take advantage of the new opportunities that came my way.

I contacted a person I'd recently been introduced to. He had another travel company and was interested in possibly buying my customer list. I went to a meeting with him, and, to my surprise, instead of just wanting to buy whatever was left of my business, he offered to partner up and keep me as the president of the company.

I quickly accepted, and, with this new alliance, our new company grew. Within two years, the company had already passed the million-dollar-a-year mark again.

A short while later, I was invited to join an international entrepreneur organization in which I would become a longtime member as well as one of the leaders of my chapter.

I also began to date again. Even though I was a bit rusty, I slowly but surely started to meet new women. Before the year had passed, I had met a wonderful, loving, and uplifting woman who a few years later would become my wife.

I went from being sad, highly in debt, and unenergetic to being full of optimism, positive energy, and wealth. I didn't just stop the negative chain reaction that had put me in the problematic situation; I changed direction and started planting positive seeds that triggered positive chain reactions.

Take a moment now to analyze the negative situation I experienced and how I was able to overcome and improve it. Did something magical happen, like a rich relative giving me lots of money as a gift? Did my future wife come knocking on my door even though we didn't know each other yet? Did my health start to improve by my continuing to be lazy and eat unhealthy food?

The answer is no to all those questions.

No outside factor came to my rescue. The solution came from within me. My exterior world was a reflection of my interior world. So until I focused and improved from within, my outer world remained the same.

Improving from within started the chain reaction that caused me to move and open doors to new opportunities. I decided to learn and grow, to think and see life more optimistically again, to have well-defined goals, and to align my actions with those goals. My positive thoughts and feelings, paired with aligned actions, were the major forces that brought me from zero to a life full of abundance in all aspects.

Now that I think back, those years of pain and suffering were priceless. They were full of challenges, pain, and suffering, yet I would not change them for anything. Those negative situations molded me into the person I am today—a person who would not have reached his current status if he had not lived and learned from those negative events.

We are all capable of obtaining what we want in life. We are all capable of being happy. In fact, happiness is a natural emotional state.

After overcoming those negative situations, I looked back and saw that prior to them I had been naturally implementing very powerful steps in my life. Yet I also noticed that very few people were applying those steps in their own lives.

I documented those powerful steps and what I had done to overcome the negative episode in my life. I also logged the new information I was discovering while helping clients through my seminars and coaching practice. After years of analyzing, learning, and writing all the important information down for my own personal reference, I ended up with a large amount of very powerful material. Once I began to organize it all, I decided that the information needed to be shared so that others could benefit from this knowledge as well, so I decided to write this book.

The whole process took me more than seven years. Now I have the privilege of being able to hand this information over to you.

For more information about the author, Walter Marin, please visit:
www.PositiveAttractionAcademy.com

Introduction

Life is beautiful. It is full of positive energy, love, laughter, happiness, abundance, wealth, health, and many other great things that make it worth living. Sometimes, though, we get interrupted by outside circumstances that make us lose focus on what is really important to us, what makes us happy, and what we truly desire.

The Positive Attraction System will allow you to identify what is best for you and bring that into your life.

It is important to understand that there is no need to wait or get anything additional to begin the process. You already have everything you need in order to start improving your life right now and get what you desire. The power is within you. When you generate positive thoughts and feelings about your desires and align your actions with them, the results will be positive every single time.

Positive Attraction contains a variety of topics that can be seen as pieces of a puzzle. Put them together to enjoy a life full of success, health, wealth, love, and happiness. Such a life is available to you. The pieces you obtain from this book will fit perfectly in the areas you need them most. Each one will get you closer to obtaining all that you desire and is best for you.

Here's an important fact: you are and have today what you thought of and did in the past. Therefore, you will be and have in the future what you are thinking of and doing now. If you are doing the same things you did in the past, you will have the same results in the future. If you change what you think of and do today in a positive way, your future will improve as well.

Your current thoughts and actions are molding your future.

You may be feeling sad or lonely. Maybe you are sick, deeply in debt, or in a troubled relationship. Or you simply want to reach your desires faster. Regardless of your current situation, you have the power within you to improve your life, starting right now. Become healthier, financially secure, happier and have better relationships by applying the power of Positive Attraction.

Every one of us can improve our own lives; we just need to know how to do it and apply that knowledge by taking action.

This book took seven years to write and to get into your hands. It will guide you, step by step, and help you reach your desires in an easy-to-understand, fun, and interactive way.

CHAPTER 1

Prepare Yourself to Attract All That Is Best for You

*Whatever is best for me, my positive thoughts
and actions will make it be.*

Always be truthful with yourself. You are the one reading this book right now, no one else. It doesn't matter what anybody else thinks. In fact, it rarely does. The only thing that matters right now is what you think.

Being honest with yourself is an essential step in improving your life and attracting what you desire. Accept that you are the main creator of the life you have today. This includes all the good things and all the seemingly bad things.

You might say, "No, my life is run by external factors. My life isn't how I want it to be; it is how it just came to be."

Well, if you trace the major decisions in your life, most of them were yours.

For example, the type of classes you took, the college you went to (or didn't go to), where you started working, what kind of friends you socialized with, whom you dated, whom you married, whom you didn't marry, and so on—those were ultimately your decisions.

When you accept responsibility for your current situation, you automatically accept that you are in control and thus able to create a better life for yourself.

Sometimes it's not easy to do, but the more truthful you are with yourself, the faster you will overcome your hurdles and reach your goals and desires.

It might take time to accept full responsibility for your current situation. Learn from this book, and take back control of your life so you can create the life you have always wanted.

When you believe your life is being run by external factors, it will be. When you believe your life is being run and controlled by you, it will be. Yes, you can still use the Positive Attraction System even if you have doubts that you are responsible for your current situation, but it will work best when you are honest with yourself.

If you don't take control of your life, life can take control of you. Acceptance instantly gives you more power and control. The more you accept the more control you will have.

Seven Easy Steps for Success

This book is full of powerful information that is organized into seven major steps that will help you attract what you want. The seven steps required for the Positive Attraction System to work at its fullest are: define desire, think, take action, feel, visualize, have faith, and receive.

Even though a few of these steps might happen at the same time, for easier understanding, we will put them in the order in which they should be followed. In the following diagram, you can see how the steps flow in the Positive Attraction Success Spiral.

Figure A-1: Positive Attraction Success Spiral

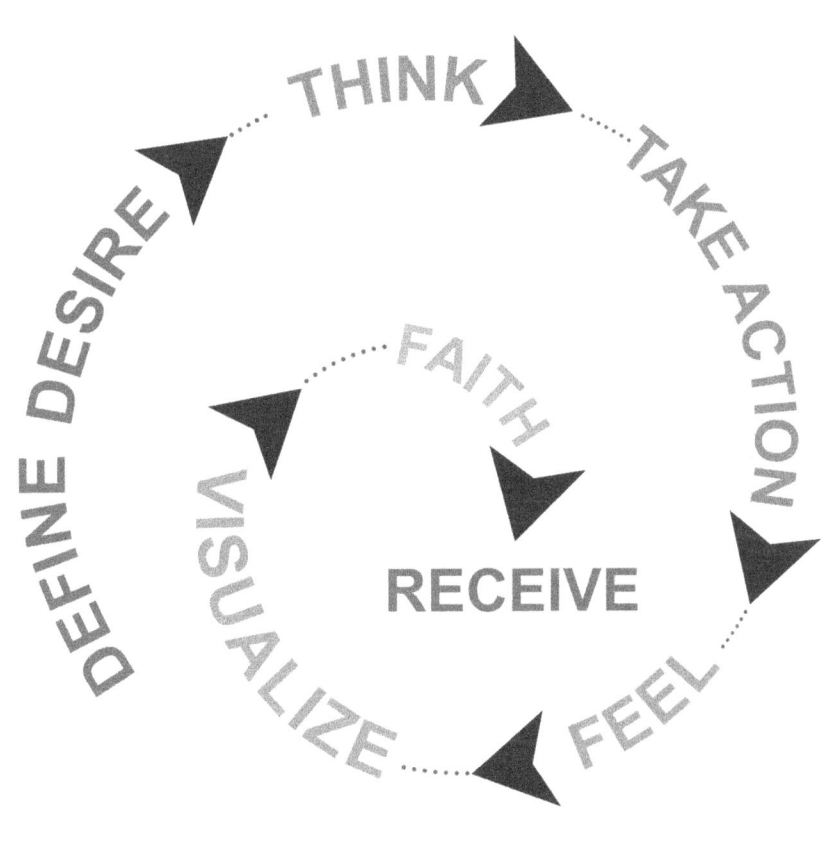

Notice that five of the steps of the Positive Attraction System are usually mental. Only two—*take action* and *receive*—are physical.

Even though many of the steps are mental and simple to follow, the improvements they bring about can be life changing.

The Positive Attraction System Circle of Power

An effective way to understand the frequency with which the steps should be repeated is by thinking of the process as a flowing circle of power.

Figure A-2: The Positive Attraction Power Circle

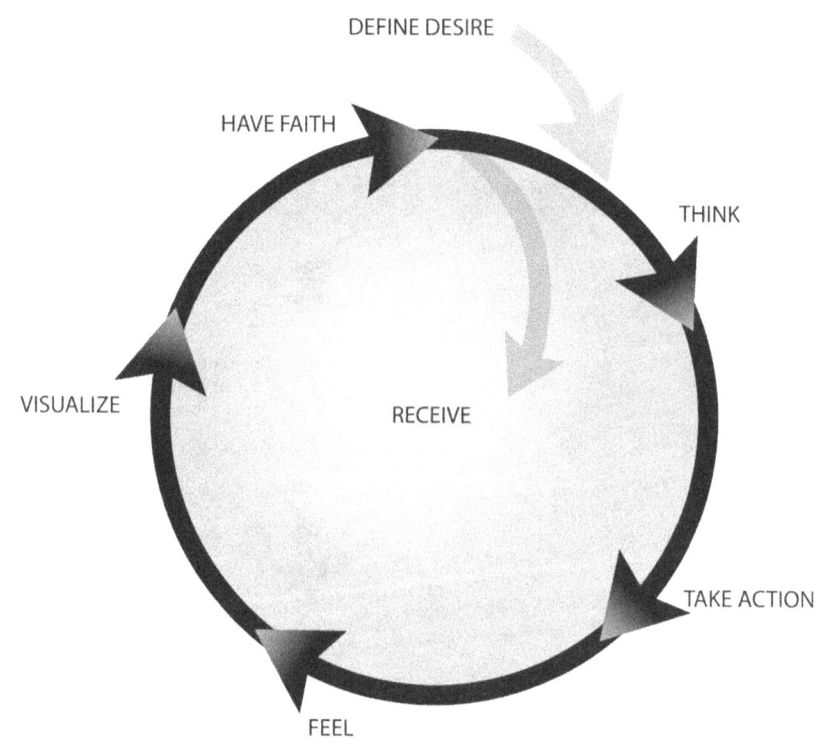

In the figure above, the first step, define desire, and the final step, receive (what you desire), are separate from the other steps in the ring because they only happen once. Once you've identified and defined your desire, that step is done. And when you receive what you desire, that step only happens one time and completes the entire process.

On the other hand, the rest of the steps in the circle can occur many times. In fact, the more often the steps are done, the closer you will get to your goal.

Please note that each step is unique, and some will be repeated more often than others. For instance, you might not take action until you have repeated other steps in the circle numerous times. Since many steps take place in the mind, they can be repeated easily.

How Important Is Each Step?

Every step in the Positive Attraction System is important in its own way. The following diagram provides an estimate of the relative importance of each step.

Figure A-3: Positive Attraction System Steps—Amount of Importance

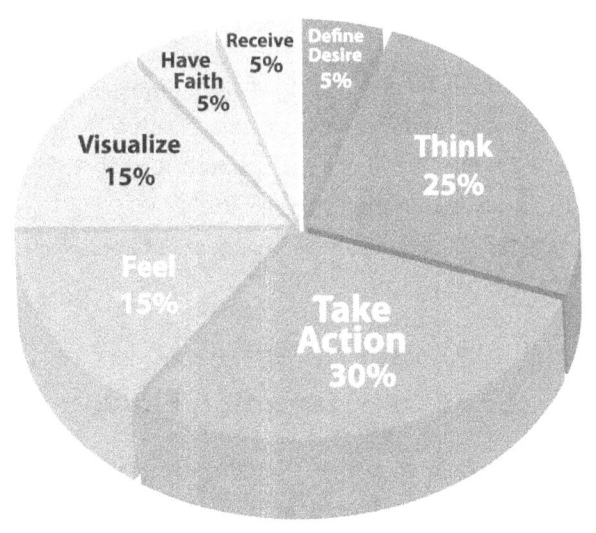

As you can see, the most important steps in the Positive Attraction System are to think and to take action. Just by thinking and taking action, you may complete more than 50 percent of the process. When you apply the rest of the steps, the possibility of obtaining what you desire is greatly improved, and the time it takes for you to receive it is greatly reduced.

The Law of Attraction

Positive Attraction uses the law of attraction as its basic building block and grows from there. In essence, the law of attraction states that like attracts like and that by having positive or negative thoughts, you bring about positive or negative results, respectively.

The law of attraction is unbiased; it doesn't take sides or differentiate between good and bad desires. It is always working, whether you are thinking of and attracting positive things or negative things into your life.

The law of attraction is mostly based on an intangible process that uses your thoughts to attract what you desire. On the other hand, Positive Attraction gives you more control by using your thoughts together with your actions and other powerful tools to attract more easily and effectively what you desire.

Simply put, Positive Attraction is the system of focusing positive thoughts and actions in order to bring about positive results. By implementing this simple yet effective process, you can realign your life toward your desires and bring immediate positive changes into your life.

Positive thoughts and actions always bring about positive reactions.

Positive Attraction System—From Tiny Seed to Blossoming Flower

Thoughts and desires are very similar to seeds. The type of seed you plant determines the kind of plant that will grow.

If you plant weeds, your garden will be full of weeds.

If you plant beautiful flowers, your garden will be full of beautiful flowers.

Think of weeds as negative thoughts, feelings, and actions while flowers are positive thoughts, positive feelings, and positive actions. What you think, what you feel, and what you do are the most important factors in determining what type of life you will have.

Following are the seven steps in the Positive Attraction System, each represented by a main ingredient required for the creation of a blossoming flower:

1. Define desire = seed
2. Think = planted seed
3. Take action = water
4. Feel = soil
5. Visualize = sunlight
6. Have faith = vitamins
7. Receive = blossoming flower

Figure A-4 : Proper Ingredients to Achieve Your Desire

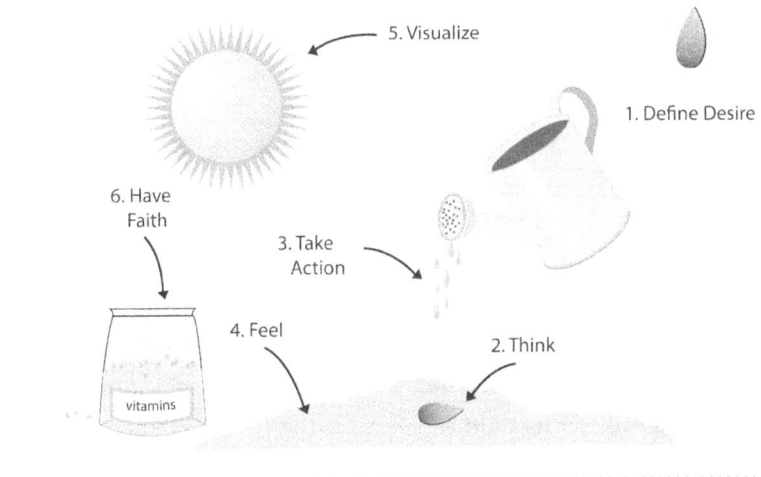

The more nutritious the soil (powerful feelings toward what you desire), the brighter the sun (vivid visualization), and the more nourishing the vitamins (stronger faith), the faster and healthier the plant will grow and blossom. These main ingredients combine to foster growth; if you eliminate a few of them, the flower will grow very slowly or not at all.

Figure A-5 : Your Desire Has Come to be, Receive It With Open Arms

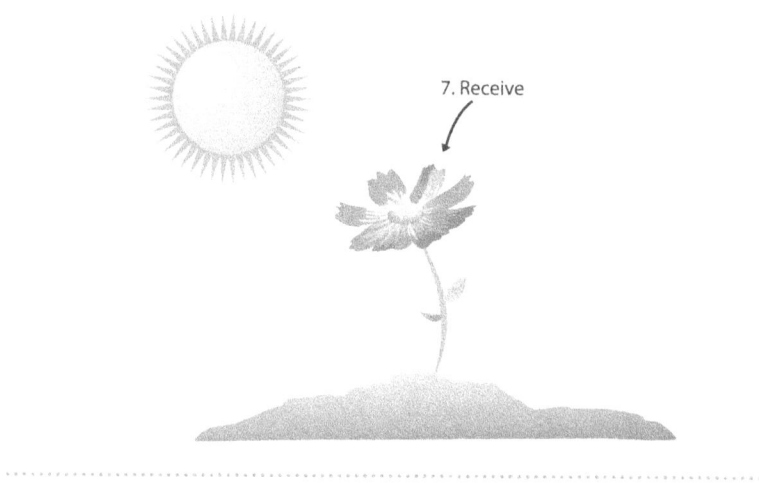

When you plant a seed (desire) in your mind, it will grow (manifest) in a certain amount of time. Depending on how well you perform the steps and how beneficial the desire is for you, it can manifest within minutes, hours, days, weeks, months, or sometimes years. Rarely will you know for certain how long it will be before you receive what you desire. For this reason, it's important to always think positively about what it is you want and the likelihood of eventually obtaining it.

Let's say, for example, that you are a couple of weeks from receiving what you desire, but you don't know that it's just around the corner. You might start to worry and think negative thoughts, doubting it will come to fruition. This starts to push your desire away from you, repelling instead of attracting it, and causing the work you have done to slowly disappear.

Despite the length of time it takes, always think positive thoughts about your desires. They are the seeds that you will someday harvest.

What Happens If I Apply Only a Couple of the Steps?

When you only apply a few of the ingredients of the Positive Attraction System to your desires, it may still work once in a while. However, the process will likely take longer to complete or produce mediocre results.

It is very difficult to reap a harvest if all you do is plant a seed. If you do not take action or take any other steps, the results will be infrequent and sporadic. Applying all of the steps is always a more powerful and effective way to attain your desires in the shortest amount of time.

If you want to take control and increase the likelihood of obtaining your desires, then you need to plant the seed, follow the steps, and, most importantly, take action. The end result will be a healthy and abundant harvest.

In life, you don't get something for nothing. The more you put in, the more you will receive. The key to success is applying all of the ingredients so that the Positive Attraction System to work at its best.

Positive Attraction
Step #1: Define Desire

CHAPTER 2

Positive Attraction Step #1
What Do You Really Want?
Define Your Desire

*Goals and desires are similar to directions on a map;
without them, you don't know which way to go.*

Desires are things we want but don't already have. The first step in the Positive Attraction System is to know what you want by clearly defining your desire. You need to know where you are going in order to get there.

How to Correctly Choose What to Attract

Make sure that what you desire is truly the best for you. Nobody knows you better than you do. Dig deep: don't want something just because you think you do or because other people want it. Following the herd won't help you find what's best for you.

Using visualization techniques can help you determine what you want. Close your eyes and visualize yourself obtaining your desire. Do your positive energies grow and make you feel good when you think about it? Use your feelings as a thermostat, and let them help you find which desire feels the most positive. Your feelings will assist and guide you in accurately defining your desires.

If what you are asking for is something that honestly makes you feel good and happy, then it is a worthwhile pursuit. If it doesn't produce any positive feelings or you even feel bad about it, then you should probably rethink what you want until you choose something that creates a better reaction inside of you.

Be completely honest with yourself. Don't say it feels good if you know deep down that it doesn't. What you feel deep down inside is the truth, and it's always best to follow your true feelings.

How to Know If What You Desire Is Best for You

When you are trying to achieve your desire, the process should be smooth. Normally you should experience a small amount of friction while trying to obtain it. If you do experience a large amount of friction, however, that doesn't necessarily mean you should stop giving your all to get what you want. It just means that you should keep your eyes open and take note if a lot of negative events begin to add up while you are trying to get what you desire.

Once in a while, you will need to overcome obstacles that will help you grow and learn before you are able to obtain what you desire. Yet if negative events keep piling up one after another, it's a good idea to stop, analyze why those negative events are happening, learn from them, and see what other options exist to obtain your desire. Also reconfirm that your desire is as beneficial as you initially thought.

During the process of trying to publish *Positive Attraction*, and after more than seven years of hard work, I was almost at the finish line. I was just a month from reaching the date that I'd set so that the book would be published and available in stores before Christmas. I had the edited manuscript, I had the company that was going to print the books, and I had some of the marketing ready to go. But something just didn't feel right.

I was still adding information to the book, proofreading, and modifying it. Also, in order to have the book reviewed, I would have to submit the copy at least three months in advance, and sticking to my original deadline would not allow time for this.

Regardless of what I did, I was being blocked in all directions.

Even though I was the one pressuring myself to reach the goal of finally publishing my book after working on it for more than seven years, it seemed that everything was against publishing it by the date I'd chosen.

After many days of nonstop work, writing and editing from the early morning when I woke up to late at night, I was completely exhausted. Meeting my self-imposed deadline was still possible, but I decided to postpone the launch date for a few more months.

I made the decision late one night after a full fourteen hours of working on the book. Immediately I felt as if a huge weight had been lifted off my shoulders. Yet a part of me also felt very disappointed. My excitement about publishing the book quickly dissipated, bringing me down and lowering my energy level. The combination of being very tired, doubting whether all my work had been worthwhile, and accepting that I wasn't going to see my book published and in my hands until March made me feel terrible.

The next morning, though, when I woke up, I felt very different. For the first time in a long while, I wasn't rushed to get my writing completed. I was able to wake up a little later and sleep well, allowing my body and mind to recuperate from the previous late nights. When I remembered that I had made the decision to postpone my book's publishing date, I immediately felt a boost of energy that brought a smile to my face. I went from having low energy and feeling down the day before to being motivated again and feeling great about the change.

My mind started to plan how to use all that extra time. I now had time to finish writing my book at my own pace again, to have it edited, and to send it out for reviews. I also had time to continue helping and coaching people, posting interesting blogs, making videos, and more.

Everything made sense again, and all the thoughts of what I had to do increased my energy level instead of depleting it the way they had before the decision.

I also realized that twice as much work needed to be done in regard to marketing that would take the same amount of time that I had postponed the launch of the book, confirming that my decision had been the correct one.

My inner power confirmed that I had chosen correctly and was heading in the right direction by creating a euphoric state of positive emotions in me.

The Happiness Circle

All that you desire and makes you happy can be traced back to three basic categories: love, health, and wealth.

Figure A-6: Happiness Circle—All Desires Fall Into 3 Categories

As you can see in the figure, the greatest of the three factors is love. By maintaining good relationships, you will have a life full of love, and you will be healthier and better able to attract more wealth into your life.

Love increases your positive energy from within and plays a major part in the amount of happiness you have. Love is any type of deep relationship with another person. This can be with a spouse or partner, a sibling, a parent, a child, an aunt or uncle, a cousin, a good friend, and so on. Love is limitless, which means that happiness is limitless.

Health is all you are physically made of here on earth and is the second most important of the three.

Everything that you desire that doesn't pertain to relationships (love) or your physical body (health) falls into the category of wealth. Wealth increases and maintains your energy from the outside in.

Each category has a direct effect on the other and all are interrelated. While love is limitless, there is a maximum state of health you can reach. In regard to wealth, even though it is essentially limitless, you can reach a certain point when adding more wealth won't increase your overall happiness. Once in a while it's common to hear of a very wealthy person that has all the material things they could ever want, yet deep down inside they are miserable. Their life is lacking strong and loving relationships with friends and family, keeping them from living a balanced lifestyle and achieving true happiness.

The more love and better relationships you have in your life, the more positive a person you will be, resulting in better health and an increased ability to attract more wealth. The wealthier you are, the more you can invest in a healthy lifestyle and the less money related issues you may experience in your relationships. The healthier you are, the clearer your mind will be and the more energy you will have to be able to attract more wealth.

The list of how they interact goes go on and on; what matters is that you know they are interrelated. If one increases, it can pull the others up. If one decreases, it can pull the others down.

The best scenario is to be balanced and have an abundance of all three. The more you have, the happier you will be and the more you and the people in your life will benefit.

I'm Not Sure What My Desire Should Be—What Should I Do?

We are here on earth to be the best we can be at what we enjoy and are good at. The better we are at it, the more the world will benefit from our talents, and the more we will be rewarded.

If you are not sure what you want to bring into your life yet, begin with small desires.

Test different paths until you find the one that is right for you. Remember, just because you chose a certain direction doesn't mean you can't change it later. It's like driving a car when you are lost. Sometimes you have to turn many times in different directions in order to find out where you are and where you should go.

Reaching small desires will guide you to where you want to be, even if you don't yet know what that final destination is.

You will be following a small ray of light that will get brighter and brighter the closer you get to what you truly desire. Eventually, you will plainly see exactly what it is you want. Also remember that your desire doesn't always have to be something major. You can apply the Positive Attraction System to anything, no matter how big or small it might be.

Stuck Between Two Choices

Sometimes we feel stuck between two major options. When you have to make a choice and you are undecided, let some time pass so you can absorb and compare all the information. As you analyze the options, remember to consider the feelings each option produces inside of you.

A client of mine was a very intelligent woman who spent most of her days studying for what seemed to be a never-ending number of college degrees. On one occasion, she couldn't decide whether to study medicine at a university in Canada or one in France.

Both options would result in the same degree, yet the option in France would require her to learn French for the admissions exam and all the courses at that university. This wasn't a major obstacle for her: she made it very clear to me that learning the new language would not be difficult for her to accomplish.

When I asked her what she preferred, she quickly replied that she didn't know. She told me the good and bad points about each but always came to the conclusion that she liked and disliked each option the same.

In fact, her whole life seemed to be like that. She had a boyfriend that she "kind of" liked to be with. She admitted that she really wasn't happy with him but didn't want to break up, either.

Any option was equally good in regard to important matters in her life. In other words, she didn't want to change, so instead she put off making any type of important decision in her life until the very last moment.

She seemed to be halfway on everything, not wanting anything to be altered. Yet deep down she yearned for something to come to her rescue and magically improve her life.

Regarding what university to choose, I asked her to visualize herself already studying and living in Canada and then in France. She closed her eyes and visualized everything about each option: how comfortable she would be communicating and taking classes in English or French, how she would feel about the short or long flights back home when visiting her parents, how she would feel to receive the degree from each university, and so on.

Each question I asked made her feel and emotionalize those specific situations.

Once she compared the possible scenarios this way, her uncertainty quickly faded.

After a couple of days of letting her decision fully soak in, she was confident of what she wanted and took action in order to make it happen.

In life-changing decisions, it's always best to let your mind ponder the possible scenarios for a good amount of time so that your thoughts and emotions fully align with the correct choice. Let the amount of positive energy and feeling you experience serve as a meter that will help you choose what is best for you at that time.

Life offers many options. Choose the best one for you by using visualization and listening to your inner power. You can choose to bring into your life whatever you desire. Choose wisely.

Write Down Your Desires

When you define, you begin to align your life.

Once you have defined what you want, writing down your goals and desires is one of the first steps toward achieving them. This will often be the first action you take, creating a chain reaction of well-defined future actions and getting you closer to your desires. Start molding and realigning your life today to live it tomorrow.

Very few people actually write down their goals. Yet those who do end up being far more successful at attaining them than those who don't.

You can start with easy desires that you want right now and then continue by adding other short-term and long-term goals. What do you want in a few months, in a year, two years, five years, and ten years? The passing of time is one of the few certainties in life. It's important to know what you want in the short and long term in order to bring your life into alignment.

Write down all of the desires you've defined. When you define, you align. With that simple yet powerful act, you will be much closer to attaining them.

Positive Attraction
Step #2: Think

CHAPTER 3

Positive Attraction Step #2
Think: It's All in Your Head

Power comes through repose; it is in the Silence that we can be still, and when we are still, we can think, and thought is the secret of all attainment.

—Charles F. Haanel

Thoughts are everything. They create everything you are, inside and out. For the most part, you are who and what you are because of what you think.

Improving your thoughts will modify your behavior; you will start to do things differently. In this way, you will be molding yourself and attracting your desires even faster.

The past is over and done. Your past experiences provide valuable knowledge, but they should not dictate your future (unless you choose to let them).

What you think of today will be your reality tomorrow, whether it's good or bad, positive or negative. You have control over your present and future.

Choosing Your Road to Success

*It is your decisions, and not your conditions,
that determine your destiny.*

—Anthony "Tony" Robbins

You can focus on many aspects of your life—the good, the bad, and anything in between. While it's normal to have a negative or insecure thought once in a while, these thoughts should be kept to a minimum.

If you are in a race and you can see the finish line in the distance, you shouldn't focus on the roads that don't lead you to the goal. Don't focus on the roads on your left or right or even the ones behind you, all of which will lead you away from your goal. Yes, other roads that lead you to different destinations do exist, and you can acknowledge them, but always keep your thoughts and actions focused on the goal.

Even though we don't have complete control of everything in our lives, we do have a great deal of control, especially over what we think and do.

As shown in the following figure, the road ahead of you is your future, the direction in which your life is heading. You are in the driver's seat, with full control over where you go, and can choose to drive in the direction that leads to your goals or anywhere else. The decisions you make today will have a direct impact on where you will be in the future.

Figure B-1: You Are in Control of the Road Ahead

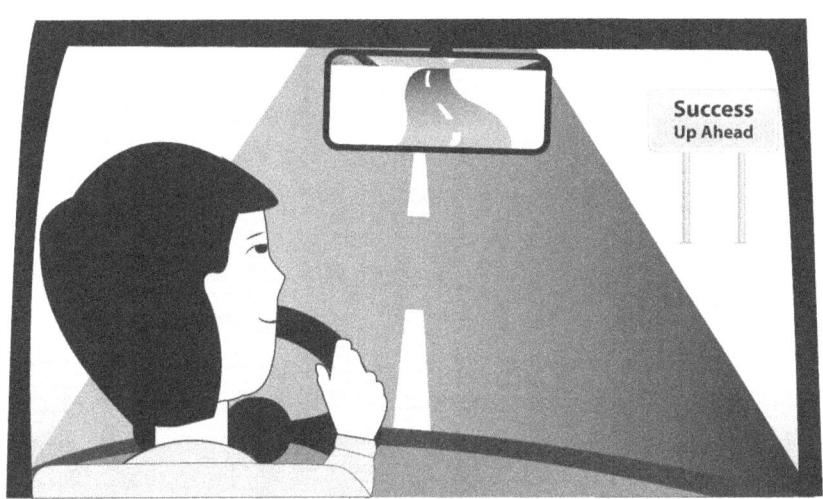

What you see in the rearview mirror is your past, the road traveled that has gotten you where you are today.

Each road behind you was a choice, and your current situation is the result of those choices.

Although your past may have created your present, what happened in your past is over. You are in control of today, tomorrow, and the rest of your life. Just because something you disliked happened yesterday, that doesn't mean it has to happen again today.

Always keep your mind and actions going in a positive direction. If you happen to go the wrong way, simply acknowledge your error, learn from it, and adjust your direction. Every so-called failure gets you closer to success when you learn from it. Failures are lessons.

You are in control of the direction in your life. Keep moving forward and realign your life in the direction that is best for you.

Remember, what you did in the past created what you are today, so what you do today creates what you will be in the future.

You Have the Power to Attract Negative or Positive

You are the only person who thinks in your mind!
You are the power and authority in your world.

—Louise L. Hay

When you are thinking a positive or negative thought and concentrating on it, something interesting happens. You start to radiate positive or negative energy that affects your surroundings and everybody you interact with. This causes you to attract not only what you think, but you also attract unrelated positive or negative events into your life.

Let's say your thought is negative. You will head down a negative path and experience negative events as well. You open your life possibilities to experiences consistent with your thoughts and actions.

Strong negative thoughts cause you to radiate negative energy and you will experience negative events. If you have sad thoughts, you will head in a negative direction and act in a way that will attract additional sad events into your life. If you have thoughts full of hatred, you will head in a negative direction and act in a way that will attract events full of hatred into your life.

This happens with positive thoughts as well. Any type of positive thought brings your body's vibration up, causes you to radiate positive energy, and you will experience positive events. If you have positive thoughts of wealth and money, you will head in a positive direction, attracting events full of wealth and abundance into your life. If you have loving thoughts, you will attract events full of love into your life. And if you have happy thoughts, you will attract additional happy events into your life.

Tune your energy level to that of what you desire by thinking positive thoughts about it. Ignore or don't take seriously any negative thoughts that might change your vibration level so they don't affect you.

You can start practicing by thinking about your desires and being grateful for what you have now. This will bring your positive energy level up so you can radiate positive energy and attract all that you deserve. Remember that in the realm of living energy, like attracts like, whether it's positive or negative.

As always, the choice of what you experience is up to you. It's an easy choice to make.

Negative Thoughts Are Troublesome Seeds That Grow

Remember, thoughts are like seeds that are planted, grow, and are harvested. The thoughts you have and the actions you take today will grow and develop; whether they become healthy, beautiful plants or thorny, troublesome weeds is up to you.

Many people focus on the problems in their lives. This is common, especially with problems that have a large impact, such as debt, troubled relationships, or health issues. But negative thoughts push your desires away from you because they are usually the opposite of them. They make you feel bad, and they take away your positive energy.

Figure B-2: Negative Thoughts Are Negative Seeds That Grow

If a negative thought goes through your mind and you notice it, don't worry. Brief, irregular thoughts don't tend to manifest. Try to eliminate that type of thought by either ignoring it or replacing it with a positive thought (which sometimes is simply the opposite).

For example, let's say you're worried that you are taking too long to finish an important project. You fear you won't finish on time. The opposite of that thought would be to simply think of finishing the project on time.

If it sounds easy to do, that's because it *is* easy to do. This simple procedure changes your thought pattern from negative to positive while converting the unconsciously self-imposed negative message of "I am taking too long; finishing the project on time is impossible" to a positive and goal-directed one: "I am constantly progressing on my project and will finish on time."

In fact, just reading this example of a negative thought followed by a positive replacement creates negative and positive feelings inside of you. Positive words give you power while negative words take power away. You can actually feel the difference.

If you enjoy talking about your problems and the negative events in your life, keep in mind that each time you do so, you are reliving and visualizing them in your mind, which will attract even more problems.

But if you enjoy talking about positive experiences in your life, keep it up. You are reliving them and will attract more positive experiences to your life.

The good days are happening now because you are alive right now. The past is over, and the future is not here yet. Be happy today so you can remain happy tomorrow.

How to Instantly Stop Negative Thoughts

We all have negative thoughts once in a while, yet there are various ways to stop them.

An effective and easy way to stop negative thoughts when they come to mind is simply to command yourself to stop and to start thinking of something else. It is preferable to start thinking of some of your goals and desires, but if you find that difficult, any neutral or positive thought will do the trick.

For example, if the thought "I am getting fatter" comes to mind, quickly say to yourself, "STOP." That will instantly stop that negative thought in its tracks and deter it from growing.

Figure B-3: How to Instantly Stop Negative Thoughts

1. When a sudden negative thought comes to mind

2. Think to yourself "Stop"

3. Then start thinking of a positive thought

Afterward think of the opposite, which in this case would be "I am getting thinner," or substitute a random positive thought, such as "This weekend will be fun."

You can also say, "Stop! I *am* in control of my thoughts and actions."

Also apply this technique when you see, hear, or read something you don't like. Anytime you're exposed to a negative message, you should cease from absorbing that information by thinking, "STOP."

Mentally saying the word *stop* effectively stops the thought in its tracks, blocking it from gaining momentum, and this allows a positive thought to take its place.

How to Eliminate Negative Thoughts Once and for All

An effective way to eliminate negative thoughts is to convert them to insignificant, positive, or humorous thoughts. Instead of allowing those negative thoughts to bring negative emotions, you can reduce their importance by substituting positive thoughts or even giggling when you think of them.

The mind focuses on things that bring you great pleasure or pain. When you cancel that feeling of pain from a negative thought, you eliminate that negative thought from your regular thought pattern or even convert it to a good thought.

When you have a negative thought, let that be the trigger that starts the thought process about something less important or humorous or something that will change your focus. You can take the power of the negative thought away by distracting your mind and changing your thought pattern.

For example, you can think of the beach, a sunny day, a cute baby, a puppy, a dolphin, the mountains—anything.

The purpose of this exercise is to disarm the negative thought and remove all of its power.

Positive statements you can use to replace negative thoughts include, "I'm strong," "I'm in control," "I'm powerful," "I'm happy," and "I'm energetic." You can also mix it up with positive or humorous words. The words can be the opposite of the negative thought or something totally different that gets your mind focused on something else.

If you want to diminish the strength of the negative thought and convert it to something humorous, think of things that make you smile or laugh, such as your favorite cartoon character or even the phrase "That's funny." For example, if your negative thoughts and fears concern getting fat, you can replace those thoughts with a thought of Snoopy, a smiling baby, a funny joke, or anything that brings a smile to your face.

This process relaxes the mind by letting it know that a thought like that is not important. It pushes the thought aside, slowly but surely eliminating it from your thought pattern.

The following exercise is another great way to eliminate negative thoughts. First, imagine a photograph with an image that represents the negative thought. Then imagine holding a large permanent marker and crossing out the image with a big *X*, scribbling it in until the very last trace of the image is blocked out. Now, with a pair of scissors, completely cut the unrecognizable picture into small pieces, and throw them into a blazing fire. Watch the papers quickly ignite and burn to a crisp. They burn so thoroughly that they start to disintegrate and become powdery ash. With the incoming wind, the fine dust particles blow away and disappear forever.

That thought has been uncreated and no longer exists.

You truly have the power to add or remove the thoughts that you choose, whatever method you choose.

Real Situations

If some of your negative thoughts concern a real situation you need to attend to in the future, use the following exercise to lessen the stress and worry the negative thought usually brings. Remember that when you are calm and relaxed, you make better decisions and attract better outcomes.

Make a list of positive words or phrases with which you would like to replace or associate a negative thought. For example, if the negative thought is that you will not be able to pay the rent on time, decrease the thought's negative power and convert it to a more positive one by changing the association with it. The replacement thoughts can be short, like *easy payment*, *positive rent*, or *increase income*, or you can use complete sentences: *I'm prepared*, *I have more than enough money*, *I'm in control*, and so on.

POSITIVE ATTRACTION STEP #2: THINK

Each negative thought that you replace with a positive one increases your energy level and your control and brings more happiness into your life.

Think of What You Want, Not What You Don't Want

Thinking about your desire will open a path filled with everything you need to attain it.

Most people know what they want and don't want in their lives. Most people want to be happy, not sad. They want to be wealthy, not poor. They want to be loved, not hated. They want to be healthy, not sick.

Yet if you try to obtain what you want by thinking of the opposite, you will usually get the opposite. Think of obtaining positive results, not of avoiding negative ones.

If you want to be healthy, don't say that you don't want to be sick; say that you want to be healthy instead. If you want to be wealthy, don't say that you don't want to be poor; say that you want to be wealthy. If you want to be happy, don't say that you don't want to be sad; say that you want to be happy. You get the idea.

Focusing on what you don't want won't help you get what you do want. It will only attract exactly that, what you don't want. But if you focus on what you *do* want, that's what you will receive.

Your mind brings into your life what you focus upon.

My friend Alex and I play golf once in a while, and he knows the procedure. One of the keys to a good golf game is to keep your head down and look at the ball when you swing. If you keep your head up, you either miss the ball or, more commonly, hit the ball in the wrong direction.

One day, Alex had some difficulty with his swing. He was telling himself, "Don't let your head up," yet his head kept coming up when he swung.

It was not until I suggested that he focus on keeping his head *down* (which has the same purpose but is simply rephrased) that he actually started to

59

keep his eyes focused on the ball and his head down throughout the swing. The result was that he hit the balls in the direction he intended.

What happened to Alex happens to all of us. When he told himself, "Don't let your head up," his mind ignored the "don't" and only acknowledged the "let your head up." So when he started his swing, his body acted on that command.

It is essential for you to notice what commands you are telling yourself so that you can remove the negatively oriented ones. Just by rephrasing and focusing on what you want (not what you *don't* want), you will get much better results. This practice is discussed in more detail in the Step #4 affirmations section.

Always keep your focus on what you desire.

Positive Thoughts Are Healthy Seeds That Grow

For as a man thinketh in his heart, so is he.

—Proverbs 23:7

When you see and concentrate on the good things, the bad things seem to be minimized. Most of the time, they even disappear from your mind.

Your brain works similarly to a computer: it does whatever it is programmed to do. When you program your mind with positive words, images, and information, you will get and live positive results. But if you let the outside world program your mind for you, you will be subject to the information it gives you. That will dictate what you will live, think, and do.

It is very important for you to filter and let in only the information you want. You must block or ignore the information you don't want. I never even acknowledge most of the "bad noise" going on in the outside world. I simply ignore it and focus on the good.

It is known that positive thoughts and feelings are so powerful that they convert into energy and communicate positive messages to the cells in your body. These messages reprogram your cells to become healthier and can even turn diseased cells into healthy ones.

POSITIVE ATTRACTION *STEP #2: THINK*

Let's review the basics. Your past created your present. Your present is creating your future. If you do nothing positive today, you will either remain the same or bring nothing positive into your future.

On the other hand, if you plant positive seeds every day, no matter how small they may be, you will be harvesting from your plentiful crop for the rest of your life.

Figure B-4: Positive Thoughts Are Positive Seeds That Grow

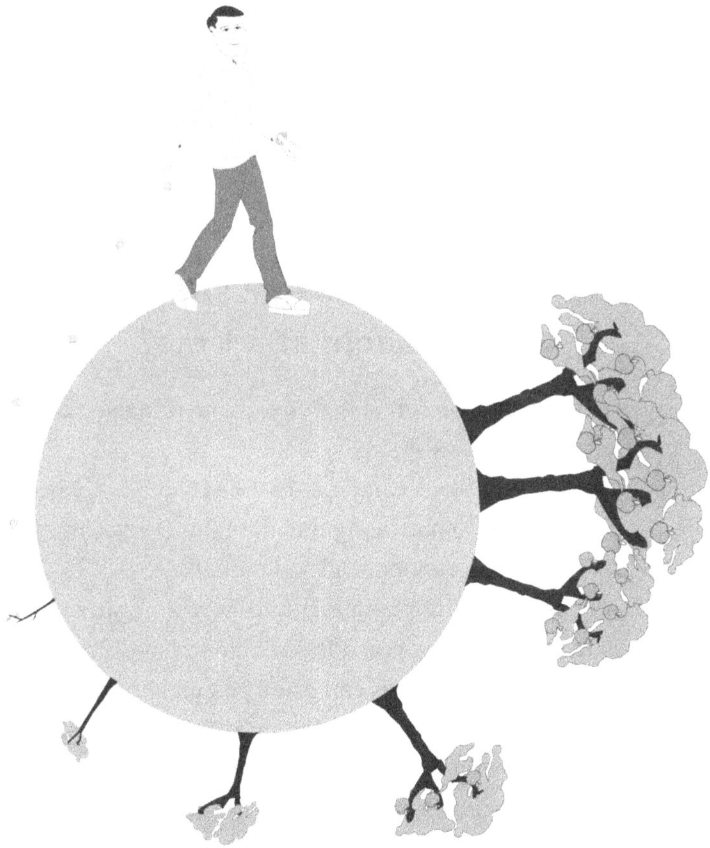

Like attracts like. The more you do, the more you get. The more seeds you plant, the more rich, abundant crops you will harvest.

Your thoughts mold your actions to bring your desires.

Neutral Thoughts

Neutral thoughts are the ones that don't affect your life in a negative or positive way. They are usually routine thoughts of present or future actions. Neutral thoughts are OK and natural to have, but there is no need to repeat them to yourself. They take up space where positive thoughts could be.

Neutral thoughts include remembering to take the trash out tomorrow, that you have to pick up groceries after work, that you have to set your alarm for eight o'clock, and so on. They exist but bring no negative or positive results to your life. A good idea is to write them down on your to-do list or enter them in your calendar and forget about them until they have to be done. This will allow you to think about your desires and other positive thoughts instead.

Did You Know You Can Only Think One Thought at a Time?

It has been proven that we can only think of one thing at a time. This phenomenon simplifies everything for us.

Your conscious mind is like a container that has room for only one thought at a time. So if we practice controlling our thoughts, replacing the bad with the good, we can essentially eliminate all bad thoughts.

Of course, it is practically impossible not to have a negative thought cross our minds once in a while. However, it is possible to have almost all thoughts be positive and let the negative ones come and go quickly and infrequently.

Remember the three types of thoughts and their consequences. Neutral thoughts have no major effect on how you feel. Negative thoughts take your energy away and make you feel sad and down. Positive thoughts give you energy and make you feel good and happy.

Figure B-5: Thoughts As Plants

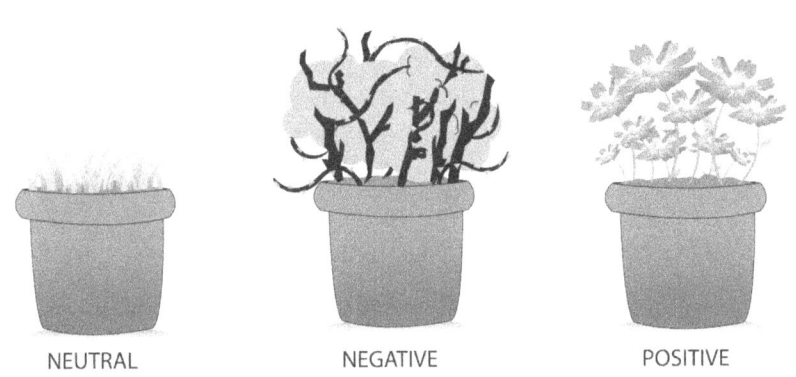

NEUTRAL   NEGATIVE   POSITIVE

The frequency of your negative or positive thoughts also plays an important part in how you feel. When you have an equal number of negative and positive thoughts during a given period, their negative and positive energies cancel each other out. The energy of the more frequent type of thought will usually dictate how you feel.

Also keep in mind that just as *what* you think is important, *how long* you think of it is critical, too. You might think five good thoughts over the course of ten minutes but think one bad thought for the next full hour. If so, that one bad thought will overpower the five good thoughts because of the length of time it was in your mind.

Controlling what you think, how often, and for how long is essential in helping you focus on positive things to reach your desires faster.

You can only think of one thought at a time. Make it a positive one.

Your Subconscious Mind: The Database of Your Life

Your subconscious mind is the major decision maker, and thus the creator, of the life you live today. It is like a database full of all the information of your life that you and your outside world have programmed and constantly continue to update.

The subconscious mind never sleeps. It controls the autonomic nervous system, which makes your heart beat, your lungs breathe, and your other organs function automatically without any assistance from your conscious mind. Even though the subconscious mind has many vital functions, I will emphasize the ones that pertain to the Positive Attraction System.

If you think about a person as a computer system, the conscious mind is the keyboard, and the subconscious mind is the hard drive. The conscious mind is used to input commands, program new information, and retrieve information stored in the subconscious mind. We live our lives based on the information stored in the database of our hard drives, so if we control and mold that information, we can control and mold our own lives.

You actively think by using your conscious mind, even though it is said to only represent about 10 percent of your brain's capacity. Your subconscious mind, on the other hand, represents the other 90 percent of your brain capacity and is much more powerful than your conscious mind.

Most of the time, you are being controlled by the instructions and beliefs embedded in your subconscious mind without even noticing it. What your subconscious believes plays an important part in whether you are happy or sad, a success or a failure, healthy or ill, and so on.

Your subconscious mind absorbs new information that your conscious mind accepts as true, and it rejects the information the conscious mind denies. Using the information it absorbs, your subconscious controls your reactions and the decisions you make in your everyday life. In other words, the data you program your subconscious mind with will determine the direction your life will take.

It's also important to know that your subconscious mind cannot differentiate between what you are actually experiencing and what you are emotionalizing and visualizing.

Even when you sit in a chair with your eyes closed and visualize what you want, your subconscious mind will think of what you are visualizing as if it's really happening. Thus visualization techniques, as well as repetition of positive words, or affirmations, work very well when you want to program your subconscious with positive information to help you obtain what you desire. These techniques will be discussed at length in the section on feeling in Step #4 and visualizing in Step #5.

The subconscious mind has another important role: it is a means of accessing the Universal Mind (also known as the Source). Your conscious mind is connected to your subconscious mind, which in turn is connected to the Universal Mind. Information is constantly flowing between them.

The Universal Mind can be thought of as a gigantic database that we are all connected to. All types of information are stored within, from the simplest to the most complex. Everything that is currently known and yet to be discovered is stored in this gigantic and magnificent database.

The connection between your subconscious mind and the Universal Mind is responsible for the ideas and answers to important questions that suddenly pop up in your mind—often called intuition, gut feelings, or hunches.

The subconscious mind has two major functions. It connects your inner power to the Universal Mind, or the Source, and it absorbs information programmed by the conscious mind, which it will later retrieve and apply to your life when needed.

Make sure the information it absorbs is coming from you, not from undesirable external sources that may be programming you with negative or erroneous commands.

If you program your subconscious with powerful positive thoughts that result in the required actions, your desires *will* become a reality. The more in touch you are with your subconscious mind, the better your life will be.

An Active Conscious Mind Equals a Less Accessible Subconscious Mind

*When you quiet your conscious mind,
your subconscious mind comes alive.*

The more active your conscious mind is, the less accessible your subconscious mind can be, and vice versa. Levels of brain wave activity define which of the two minds is more accessible.

When you are wide-awake, and your mind is active and alert, you brain is considered to be in beta state. When you are calm, relaxed, and your mind is quiet, your brain is considered to be in alpha state.

When you are alert and thinking and having voluntary thoughts, your conscious mind is more active. When your conscious mind becomes less active, your subconscious mind wakes up and is able to receive and give ideas that come from your inner power.

The manner in which your minds communicate with each other is a one-way street. Your conscious mind can tell or ask your subconscious what it wants, but while it is doing so, the subconscious can only listen. The same occurs when the subconscious communicates with the conscious mind.

One of the best times to focus and visualize is when your mind is relaxed or drowsy since that is when it goes into alpha state, and your conscious mind is slowed. When your conscious mind is relaxed, it will open up and give the subconscious mind access. This permits your subconscious mind to be more awake and accessible. This is also the best time for the conscious mind to tell the subconscious mind what it wants.

Sometimes when we want an answer to a question from the subconscious mind, we try to force it to communicate. The subconscious, however, can't be forced. When it is, two outcomes typically occur: either you don't receive an answer, or the answer you do receive most likely originated in your conscious mind, which oftentimes is incorrect. Subconscious ideas come naturally, without force.

It takes practice to know how to differentiate effectively between the two. Subconscious ideas are pure and emerge naturally while conscious ideas are usually forced and biased, telling you what you want to hear.

At certain times of the day when your conscious mind is calm and not occupied with other thoughts, you can more easily listen to your subconscious.

For example, when I am at my office during the day, it can be very hard to access my subconscious because I am busy working on my computer, receiving calls, being interrupted by coworkers, receiving chats, and so on. Such distractions keep the conscious mind occupied and keep subconscious thoughts from being accessible.

You should balance your time and include some time to relax and connect with your subconscious mind each day.

A Clear Mind Brings Clear Thoughts

While you work, go to school, do homework, or worry about routine chores such as paying your bills or taking the kids to school, you are not allowing yourself time to relax and have clear, pure thoughts. Your mind is likely focused on environmental stimuli or events in your life, and this prevents it from receiving positive and life-enhancing thoughts.

Tapping all the great benefits your inner power has to offer is difficult when you are constantly being distracted. You need to slow down and take a step back in order to get in touch with your inner power. Clear your mind and allow yourself to think and focus on your truly important questions and desires.

The more disconnected you are from the outside world, the more connected you will be to your subconscious mind. Meditation, which is discussed in the section on visualization in Step #5, is one of the best ways to clear your mind.

You Are What You Think:
Reprogram Yourself for Success

In addition to absorbing information we agree with, the subconscious mind absorbs information that is repeated to us many times. When you hear, see, or read the same thing over and over again, your subconscious starts to absorb that information.

After a certain number of repetitions, your subconscious will accept a message as true and store that information in its database. That is why you should avoid negative information from any source. Negative information brings you down and creates negative thoughts and feelings.

When we were young, many of our parents unknowingly programmed our subconscious minds with negative thoughts. Many times we carried these thoughts into our adult years, thoughts like, "You are a bad boy" or "You are not good at that." Or we were programmed with negative commands like "Don't do that."

Luckily, we can reprogram our subconscious minds. We can correct those and any other ingrained negative thoughts and replace them with positive ones. Remember, you control what your subconscious thinks by accepting or denying the information given to it.

You should reject and block information you don't agree with. Make sure you don't start believing something you know is untrue just because it is being repeated to you from outside sources. Rejecting information is simple: after reading, hearing, or watching any type of information you don't agree with and don't want your subconscious to accept, you can simply say to yourself, "That's not true," "I don't believe it," and "No."

Conversely, you should allow yourself to absorb positive information and program your subconscious to accept whatever you desire. You can use repetition to reprogram yourself to think, act, and live exactly the way you want to.

- If you want to be happy, think happy thoughts.
- If you want to be healthy, think of health, strength, and purity.
- If you want to be wealthy, think of abundance: making lots of money, having a big savings account, and gaining financial stability.
- If you want to have a loving relationship, think of love, happiness, and sharing.

The more often you think about your desires, the more powerful those thoughts will become. The more often you repeat them, the more deeply they will be absorbed by your subconscious, which will bring about aligned actions and allow you to obtain your desires much more rapidly. Additional information on positive reprogramming can be found in the section on affirmations in Step #4.

Bring Down Your Mental Barriers!

Most of the things that block you from reaching your desires are neither tangible nor brought about by external circumstances. They are self-imposed mental barriers created by you in your mind.

Sheila was a woman who had very low self-esteem, didn't think she could accomplish much in her life, and always talked down to herself. She had tried to improve her situation a few times and failed. As a result, she was very afraid of trying and failing again.

It wasn't until I helped Sheila accept that having failed in the past didn't mean failure in the future that she gave herself the opportunity to take action and try again. She learned that every failure offers something beneficial and that each of her failures contained a lesson that could be applied to her future experiences.

I also made her aware of how negatively she talked to herself. She constantly put herself down, which kept her positive feelings and energies from growing. We worked on cleaning up her negative internal talk and slowly but surely replaced it with motivational and positive phrases. Just by replacing the negative messages she gave herself, she increased her self-confidence.

After a short while, she was able to bring down her self-imposed mental barriers and give herself a chance. Gradually, her world started to improve, and she began to attract many of the positive things she desired.

What had happened to Sheila? Due to several failed attempts to improve her life, her subconscious was programmed to believe that she couldn't achieve her desires, that the results would always be the same. This belief caused her to erect self-imposed mental barriers and fears, which made her feel powerless.

This happens to all of us at some point. You need to overcome mental barriers by eliminating your fears and accepting that a failed attempt in the past doesn't necessarily mean failure in the future.

You deserve to have exactly what you desire. Bring down those mental barriers, and start improving your life today!

Correctly Associate Pleasure and Pain

The associations you have with everything you interact with determine your reactions to them. It is very important to realize that your actions depend on how much pleasure or pain you associate with things in your life.

The more predominant and powerful emotional response will drive your decisions.

Most people's associations are incorrectly set up and therefore bring negative results into their lives. If, for example, you want more money in your life, but you think of money as the root of all evil or that people who have lots of money are greedy, you are associating money with something negative, and you will subconsciously push money away from your life. If you think love hurts, you are welcoming pain into your relationships. If you think exercise makes you sweat too much and smell bad, you will find it hard to do.

Attach strong positive emotions to what you like and what is best for you. But don't stop there. It is also *very* important to attach strong negative emotions to what is not beneficial to you and what you want to remove from your life. Analyze the consequences of the actions you take, and associate them with pain and pleasure accordingly.

The following are some common activities and their appropriate associations, either pain or pleasure. Elaborate on the descriptions of each of those you need to work on, and add new ones that pertain to your life.

1. Exercise: pleasure
   View exercise as a mini vacation. Think about getting away from your daily work routine, lowering your stress level, becoming more attractive to the person you like, feeling better, having more energy, and so on.
2. Saving money: pleasure
   Saving can grant us peace of mind, serve as insurance for unforeseen events, and be a money magnet. Money generates positive energy and attracts more money.
3. Accumulating debt: pain
   Having too much debt creates large amounts of stress and takes your positive energy away.
4. Eating junk food: pain
5. Eating natural foods: pleasure
6. Cleansing your body: pleasure
7. Being lazy: pain
8. Giving compliments: pleasure

9. Criticizing people: pain
10. Being nice: pleasure
11. Being rude: pain
12. Helping someone: pleasure

Write down associations like these that make you personally feel pain or pleasure, and then expand on why they make you feel that way. Be honest with yourself. If you want to improve and reach your desires, every little thing counts. Only by being truthful about your current associations will you be able to correct any mismatched associations and get closer to your desires.

Begin to notice which things in your life give you positive energy and which take your energy away. Then modify your associations so that positive emotions are attached to beneficial things and negative, painful emotions are attached to negative ones. The more you personalize your associations, the more effective they will be.

When you change your associations correctly, your attitude improves, and you react positively to good things and negatively to bad, improving other parts of your life in the process.

Learn how to reprogram your mind with the correct associations. It's your mind; take control and mold it to think the way you want it to.

Positive Attraction
Step #3: Take Action!

Positive Attraction Step #3
Take Action!

Well done is better than well said.

—Benjamin Franklin

Thought is the spark; action, the fire.

Taking action is one of the most important parts of the Positive Attraction System. This step is physical, not mental. You convert intangible thoughts into something tangible.

Notice that the word *attraction* contains two words: *attract* and *action*.

The more important of these words is *action*. This is a key ingredient in Positive Attraction. Without action, there may be very little or no attraction.

What you do now is what creates your future, regardless of what you have lived in the past. Thinking about your desires creates the possibility for them to exist. Taking action gives your thoughts momentum and brings them into reality.

If you only think of what you want without taking action, you lose control and leave the attainment of your desire up to chance. Very seldom do things happen miraculously or magically. You have to make them happen.

Without action, desires remain in your mind. With action, they start to become reality.

Action is any interaction between you and the material world, however small it might be. It's not only what you think that will change your life.

Change depends on a combination of factors, but most important is what you *do* with your thoughts.

When you take action, you gain greater control of your life and start to attract the tools and opportunities needed to reach your desires.

Bring thoughts of what you desire out in your everyday life by means of actions to make your desires become reality.

Positive actions always create positive reactions.

Start Now by Taking Action Immediately

Do not wait: the time will never be "just right." Start where you stand, and work whatever tools you may have at your command and better tools will be found as you go along.

—Napoleon Hill

What do you want more than anything else? If you want it that badly, prove it.

The most successful people I know do things instantly. They don't procrastinate. They don't wait until something has to be done. They do it on the spot.

Small and basic tasks that don't require much thought should get done in the moment. More important tasks should be analyzed to see whether they're worth doing to get you closer to your desire. Once you see that an action will be beneficial, take it immediately.

The key to making the Positive Attraction System work is not only to *think* positively, but to *be* positive. What you think is intangible and is only the spark. Action is the fire that makes your thoughts become a reality.

The more fuel there is, the larger the fire and the better the results. The more action there is, the more reactions there will be, bringing faster and better results.

What happens when you have positive thoughts about what you desire? You get filled with positive energies and feel good. But ending the process there limits your ability to advance much further. What happens when you have a positive thought about what you desire and you follow through by taking action? Everything.

Every single successful person that exists or has ever existed has taken action in order to become a success. Success comes to those who take action, period.

The more actions you take, the more you will learn and be able to align your life toward reaching all of your desires.

I've gone to many courses (some of them very expensive), and it always amazes me how some people invest time and money to learn but don't apply that knowledge afterward. They have learned all the information they need in order to be successful, yet they don't take action.

With the passing of time, the people who applied the information start to separate from the people who didn't. The people who learned yet did nothing remained the same while the people who took action and actually applied their new knowledge not only became more knowledgeable, but they also reached their goals.

The significant factors that vary the speed with which you achieve your desires are the intensity of your thoughts and how quickly you take action. The more you think about your desires and the faster you move, the sooner you will see results.

Even if you don't succeed at first, keep trying. The only way to find out if you are heading in the right direction is to start trying. Be confident, and use the knowledge you learn when you don't succeed to adjust your actions accordingly. Every so-called failure is a lesson that will open doors and get you closer to where you want to be.

Here is a simple mathematical truth:
POSITIVE THOUGHTS + POSITIVE ACTIONS = POSITIVE RESULTS.

Actions equal change, and change equals results.

Bringing Change into Your Life Is Good

In order to attract, you need to act.

If you already are where you want to be or already know that you are heading in the right direction, you might not need to make many changes. But if you aren't where you want to be and you continue without any adjustments, you *will* keep getting the same results.

Take a minute to review your life as it is right now. Look at your what you have, where you live, the people you interact with daily, your job, your friends, your body, your mind, your level of happiness, and your life as whole.

Who you are and what you have today are the result of your past thoughts and actions. If you are already obtaining your desires and you are successful and content heading in your current direction, then keep doing so. But if you still haven't obtained your desires and feel that you are stuck, you must change. If you continue to take the same actions that got you where you are now, the reality is that if you don't change you might not reach many of your desires.

The reason is simple: if your past thoughts and actions were working to bring your desires as effectively as possible, then you should have already attained many of them by now. If you have not attained many of your desires, then some changes in your life are necessary.

If you want to improve a little, then change a little. If you want to improve a lot, then change and improve a lot in the areas that will benefit you the most. If you want to dramatically change your life, then *you* have to dramatically change first. Drastic improvements require drastic changes.

There is no set time frame: how fast or slow you go is up to you. But the faster you apply the changes in your life, the faster you will see results.

Remember that what you were doing yesterday and in the distant past is what got you to where you are today. You know what remaining the same will bring—you live it every day. If you keep doing what you are doing, you will continue to receive more of the same.

Now experience what doing something different will bring.

You have to be flexible and adapt to certain changes in order to obtain better results.

Start taking steps that get you closer to your goals, and stop doing what keeps you in the same place or pushes you away from your goals.

In order to achieve your desires, you have to take a step back and analyze what you are doing.

1. Analyze your current life situation, the good and the bad.
2. Notice which actions bring positive results and which do not.
3. Replace the actions that are not getting you closer to your desires with different actions.

To get a different result in your life, you need to change your actions. Without change, things will remain the same.

When you start taking new actions and can clearly see that they are improving your life, continue down that road. If you don't see improvement, keep repeating the previous steps until you find something that does work. Since most of the time you don't know what works until you try it, you will need to apply the trial-and-error method until you produce the results you want.

Sometimes you will need to break your routine in order to apply the changes. As long as you are improving, growing, learning, and getting closer to your goals, then change is good.

Actions—like thoughts—communicate, teach, and program your subconscious. The actions you take mold you into what you are or will become. When you break your routine and get out of your comfort zone, you may be forcing yourself to do something that is new and sometimes unappealing. It might be hard to do in the beginning, but this important step will allow you to program yourself and learn from those actions. You will be feeding your mind new information that will give you the knowledge necessary to open paths that take you where you want to be.

I have had many school- and work-related changes in my life and have purposefully gone in many directions. When I was in college, I loved business and traveling, so I got a bachelor's degree in international business. After that I wanted to diversify and do something more challenging, so I adjusted my direction again and obtained a financial planning certificate and then a master's degree in finance.

I have realigned and reinvented myself many times in my career as well. In high school I managed my mother's restaurant and later my father's movie theatre. During college I worked for many years in a bank, in telemarketing, in multilevel marketing, and in a jewelry store. I was also a guide and a featured extra in *Titanic*, as well as being in the production side of that and another major movie.

After I graduated, I didn't want to get a regular job for a financial company, so I decided to create my own businesses. Creating a business is like being a first-time parent. Everything is new, and every day is a learning experience. My new businesses were in very different industries, which required me to learn great amounts of information in order to be successful. I have always strongly believed that you get out what you put in, so I always give my all in everything I do.

I created several types of businesses, including a website-design company, an online and physical travel company, and a telecommunications company. Now I write books, coach individuals and business owners, give seminars and speak at conferences.

None of these changes would have been possible had I not been flexible and open to going in the different directions that new opportunities guided me toward. All the changes served as lessons, bringing me large amounts of knowledge and guiding me to where I am now.

If you removed any of those experiences, the good or the bad, I would not be the person I am today.

Small Changes to Your Daily Routine Bring Huge Results

Small changes can be very powerful. Over time, they compound, grow, and create large changes.

Think about what happens when you slightly move the steering wheel of a car when you're driving. If you are driving straight and move the steering wheel by a very small amount to either side, that small change over time and distance will have a huge effect on the direction you are heading toward and your final destination.

Sometimes you may find yourself running in circles in your daily routine, doing the same things over and over again and attracting the same results. Remember, you are the creator of that routine. Although routines can be positive, some daily routines may be neutral or negative and may be preventing you from redirecting your life toward a positive direction.

More effort will be required to change directions because you will be breaking from your normal routine and heading toward a new one. You may be moving away from your comfort zone, and you will need to adapt in order to create momentum and improve your life. Still, even if the changes you make are small, they can bring big results into your life.

When you are given opportunities and have the option to take action, you need to be flexible and open to moving in a new direction. With positive realignment, you will be growing and reaching a higher level. Once you get accustomed to heading in the new direction, you will gain momentum, and you will flow smoothly.

When you change your routine and, in turn, take actions that bring better results, your energy level instantly rises. Correct your direction and start heading toward goals you want to obtain, eliminating unwanted routines and replacing them with positive, life-enhancing ones.

Remember, if you keep doing what you are doing, you will keep getting what you are getting. Apply positive changes, and you *will* get positive results.

Get the Ball Rolling

*You don't have to get it perfect,
you just have to get it going.*

—Jack Canfield

Temporary or superficial thoughts and actions are a small push toward what you want. You need to get the ball rolling, to create momentum.

But you need to push long enough and hard enough to start moving forward. After a while, it will be easier to push since the ball will already be moving.

The biggest effort usually takes place in the beginning, which is the re-aligning stage of flowing positively. This is similar to riding a bicycle. When the bicycle is still, friction with the ground keeps it from moving. When you start, pedaling will take far more energy than when the bicycle is already moving. Starting is almost always the part that requires the most effort.

Initially, it might seem as if you are putting in a lot of effort and receiving very few or no results. That is because you are just starting to move. Greater results for your effort will come down the line.

Once you are moving at full speed, the amount of effort required to keep moving forward will be much smaller than in the beginning because you will have *momentum*. Soon the bicycle will continue to move forward in the same direction without much effort even if you stop pedaling for short periods of time.

You can also think of how momentum works by imagining a long line of dominoes placed one after another in a perfect row. When you knock down the first domino, all the others fall, one after another, with the momentum of the first.

Likewise, when you're starting to realign your actions toward your desires, the most energy is required in the beginning. Once you've started, constantly moving forward and maintaining momentum is the smoothest way to achieve your desires.

Be Proactive: Conquer Your Problems

Even though positive changes (no matter how small they might be) bring positive results, some people tend to avoid them. They prefer to submerse themselves in their daily activities in order to distract themselves from their current, and sometimes saddening, reality.

I had a client named Christian who came to me seeking help and hired me as his coach. Although he'd approached me for help with a different issue, I noticed he was living his life as if he were a robot. He was doing the daily routine he programmed himself to do and ignoring anything else that might interrupt the process, whether good or bad.

Even though his relationship with his wife was overflowing with problems and his health was deteriorating, he preferred to focus on his daily tasks rather than face what he considered to be an eternally sad and gloomy reality.

His back was turned and his eyes were closed to all of his problems. Unfortunately, this also meant that his doors were closed to any good events and opportunities that came his way. But keeping his conscious mind distracted and occupied was his way of coping with life.

His behavior was similar to that of people who try to ignore their sorrows by drinking too much alcohol. Their problems still exist, yet for a brief time, their minds are distracted, so they feel less pressure and pain.

The reality is that Christian is not a robot. He is not and will never be a cold and emotionless machine, regardless of how hard he tries to convince himself that he is. Sooner or later, I warned him, his problems would become so great that he would have to face reality. At that point, he would be forced down a road he did not choose and lose more control over his life.

Basically, he was living his life as if driving a car while looking down at his feet, ignoring the direction he was heading in. I explained to him what would happen were he to continue: when he is finally forced to look up, to his surprise he'll see that he is about to crash into a huge wall. In fact he might be so close that it will be too late to avoid.

Christian had two basic choices. He could continue to be a reactive person by ignoring his problems and then be forced to deal with much larger and painful issues in the future. Or he could become proactive and fix his issues in a faster, more effective, and painless way.

Christian chose to become more proactive and improve his life.

By opening his eyes to his reality, he was able to fix his issues at his own pace and prevent future problems. This also allowed him to remove the blinders and see all the good and positive people and opportunities that were available to him.

Once he became proactive and resolved his issues, he gained control of those situations, and his life improved dramatically.

Be proactive and start making positive changes in your life. You have nothing to lose but much to gain. Let your ambitions and desires motivate you to start improving your life today!

Problems Are Our Friends

When something "bad" happens in your life, it is usually something you need to learn from. It is a nudge that is trying to guide you in the right direction.

To most people, just thinking of the word *problem* generates some sort of stress. Yet regardless of how 99 percent of the world thinks of them, problems can truly be your friends.

At certain points in your life, you may start to experience a series of negative events, one after another. This may be an indication that you are heading in the wrong direction and need to realign. You need to correct your actions in order to head in a positive direction again.

Problems are like the different-sized bumps off to the side of the road when you are driving. If you stay on the paved road, you will be heading in a positive direction and flow smoothly.

When you drift away from your positive direction, problems alert you that you are getting off course by giving you a nudge. The intensity of the nudge will depend on how far you are drifting away from what is best for you.

If you are drifting away only slightly, the nudge will be gentle. If after many such nudges you keep heading in the wrong direction, the nudges will increase in strength (i.e., your problems will intensify).

POSITIVE ATTRACTION *STEP #3: TAKE ACTION!*

Figure C-1: Problems Are Our Friends

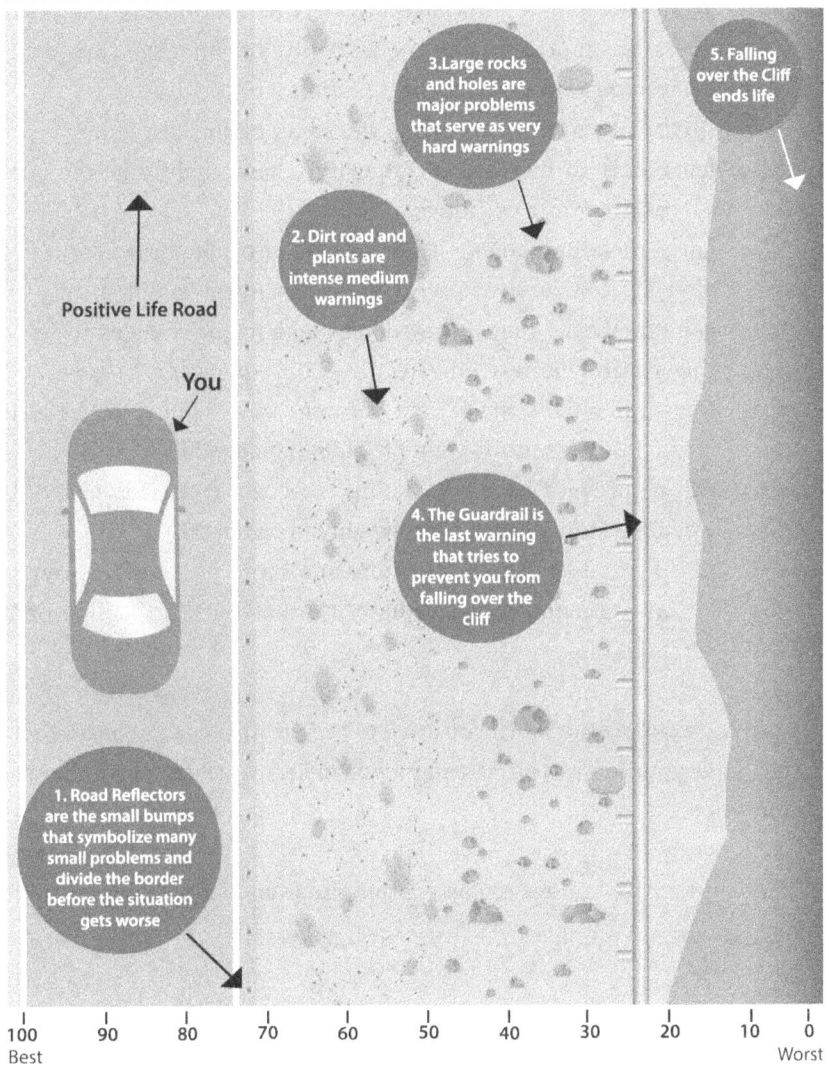

- Car = You are in the drivers seat and in control of the direction the car is heading.
- Road = The smooth and straight road symbolizes your positive life direction.

1. Road reflectors = These are small bumps that symbolize many small problems that occur in a short period of time and add up, one after another. They try to notify you that you are drifting away from your positive life direction.
2. Dirt road and plants = When the small bumps are ignored, problems start to increase in intensity. These slightly larger bumps serve as medium warnings.
3. Large rocks and holes = These are major problems, sometimes life altering, that serve as severe warnings. At this point, most people can plainly see that if they don't make major changes to realign, they face further extreme negative consequences.
4. Guardrail = This is the last warning, which will come as a hard crash. It represents a huge problem in your life that is doing all it can to prevent you from falling over the cliff. This is the final warning—the borderline between life and death.
5. Cliff = If all the small, medium, and large problems weren't acknowledged and didn't redirect the person's life, falling off the cliff ends life.

In the car example the more you stick to the positive road, which is on the left, the better your life will be. The more you drift toward the right, the worse your life will be.

There are four basic steps to correct this situation when it starts to get out of hand:

1. First, slow down or stop in order to prevent the situation from worsening. Remember that small (and, eventually, medium or large) warnings will notify you when you are headed in the wrong direction and need to correct your path.
2. Second, analyze why you are flowing negatively—why certain things are happening (or not happening).
3. Third, learn from those problems. They all have lessons to teach that you can apply to other situations.
4. Fourth, realign your actions toward a different direction that will bring you positive results.

Most problems are lessons to be learned. Only when you learn from them can you realign and overcome them. The more you are in tune with the nudges life gives you, the easier it will be to guide yourself away from the negative and toward the positive.

A few years ago, I was in a car accident at a time when many negative events were happening to me. But it took this severe and sudden negative event to make me realize that my life had recently presented many warnings. After many small and medium warnings, which I ignored, the crash was the major warning that finally made me notice, stop, and analyze my situation. It confirmed without a doubt that my life was heading in the wrong direction.

Prior to this period, my life had been stable, healthy, and happy. But I realized that in the few months prior to the accident, my life had slowly but surely realigned itself, and I had begun to head in a direction in which I did not want to go.

The major derailment began with a breakup with a woman I had dated for a while; the ensuing emotions blurred my mind and affected my decision-making process.

Then I added fuel to the fire by socializing with old acquaintances. Though I'd had things in common with them in the past, those similarities now caused me to get further off track.

I was exercising less, eating out too often, and dedicating time to superficial and unimportant things.

After the crash, I slowed down, then decided to stop my routine for three whole days and stay home (except for exercising and grocery shopping) to analyze what was happening. Even though I had other commitments to attend to, I decided that realigning my life was more important.

I knew my life was heading in a negative direction and that the decisions I had been making and actions I had been taking were wrong. The first day, I just felt horrible. Nothing in my life was making sense, and one bad thing after another was happening.

I went outside to run and walk. Being outside in the clean air always helps to clear the mind, making the subconscious more accessible to guide and help you. Exercising brought down my stress level, got the toxins out, and stabilized my brain chemicals while generating feel-good endorphins.

At the grocery store, I bought organic fruits and vegetables to make my juices. I also bought some fish and whole-grain foods. I always try to eat food that is as natural and healthy as possible, since foods alter mental, emotional, and physical states. Even though organic and natural foods might sometimes cost more, my body is worth it—and so is yours. When you pay extra for natural and healthy foods, you are investing in yourself, and you're worth every penny. The more natural foods you eat, the better you will feel and think, the brighter your inner star will shine, and the faster you will reach your desires. Everything counts in large amounts.

With the ups and downs of the past few days, I was also very tired, so I took a nap during the day to help my body regenerate.

I brought out my life plan and list of goals to review and update. I spent several hours, off and on, making sure that those desires were the best for me and applying the other Positive Attraction System steps.

If I hadn't stopped and realigned my life, it most likely would have continued to worsen, with problems piling up one after another, bringing more pain and sorrow until I listened to the warnings and lessons I was receiving.

Thanks to this major warning, I learned from my mistakes and realigned my life, getting back on track to fulfill all my desires. Shortly after this weekend, my life didn't just continue the way it had been before those major issues—it actually improved. My new perspective, drive, and clarity of my desires had raised me to another level.

Whenever something bad happens in your life, analyze why it happened. Trace it back to the root of the problem, and then extract the good from it.

It may be hard to believe, but it's true: living through a bad event and learning from it is better than not having experienced that bad event at all. Learning the important lesson a negative event has to teach can redirect your life and bring you positive results.

Resolve Your Problems ASAP

Even though problems can be helpful, when they are ignored for too long, they can grow into larger problems and continue to worsen. The longer the problem is ignored, the larger it may become, and the longer it will take to fix. The faster you address the problem, the less of a problem it will be.

The way to stop problems in their tracks is to take action and resolve the issues once and for all.

Problems can truly be seen as friends when we accept them as boundaries that try to prevent us from heading in the wrong direction while at the same time teaching us valuable life-enhancing lessons.

Realign Your Life toward Your Desires

When you truly want something, a door will be opened for you. All you have to do is walk in.

With new desires comes the need to make changes in order to realign your life and head in a new direction. Some desires will be small, and you won't need to realign much. Others will be larger and will require more re-alignment for you to reach them.

A while ago, I had to realign my life due to my new travel schedule.

I had a friend who needed someone to help coach and guide new executive members of an organization. Since I had over ten years of experience in the business organization, had served on the board, and had been for many years a leader of my groups, I was prepared to help, even though it would mean constant travel to another state.

The situation wasn't ideal. First, accepting the position would stall my plan to relocate to Texas. Plus, this new commitment would last for a minimum of six to ten months, and the travel schedule would mean I would have more expenses. (Since this was a favor to a friend and the organization, I would be paying for my own flights, hotels, meals, and so on.) It also would cut into the time I would be able to dedicate to my business and book writing.

I thought about it every day, trying to visualize the best possible scenario.

I struggled for a few days, trying to find the appropriate changes to my life that made sense and generated positive feelings inside of me, and soon I had the solution. I created a plan that would actually save money and reduce my stress level. All in all, understanding the new changes that were required, re-aligning my life, and planning the future actions took me about a week.

I accepted the offer to help, and after a few months, I realized that if I hadn't made that commitment to help, my life would have been totally different. Because I accepted, my first trip to get a new place in Austin, Texas, coincided perfectly with a trip that my girlfriend (now wife) was making with her family. This fortified our relationship, brought us closer to each other, and opened the door for us to get engaged.

This unrelated opportunity actually helped me achieve one of my major personal desires.

Also, thanks to my decision, I met several business executives, many of whom became great friends. I even ended up collaborating with one of them in a new business venture.

My overall situation improved because I'd focused on figuring out how to arrange my commitments in a way that would allow me to help the people involved. If it wasn't for that change, the course of my life and the lives of the others involved would have been very different.

Acting and Attracting

Man makes an action;
the action makes the man.

Acting is one way of taking action.

If you feel sad but act happy, you will eventually become happier.

If you don't have much money but begin to be grateful for what you do have and start acting like your life is full of wealth and abundance, you will attract just that.

Your actions mold your thoughts and reprogram your subconscious mind. By acting a certain way, you accept that what you do is correct, and your subconscious will store that information in its database for future use. You will then begin to align your life accordingly and attract more of what you are programming.

Simply put, you are—or become—what you do.

Be Confident That Good Will Come from Any Situation

I now know that I shouldn't be worried about certain situations that have the potential to cause a major disruption in my life, such as ending a relationship or losing a job. My whole life, I have always been led down the right path. Although at times I seemed to be in very bad circumstances, with hindsight I see that those events were lessons and exactly what I needed at that time. If it hadn't been for them, everything in my life would have been different.

This doesn't mean that you should do nothing and just let life work itself out. It won't. What I mean is that if you learn from a situation, think positively, and take positive actions, the results will be good. Don't just go with the flow if you see your life heading the wrong way. You have to be proactive and redirect your life. Knock down the first domino, and begin the chain of positive events. Keep guiding your life in the correct direction to the best of your knowledge: learn from any seemingly bad event, and realign your life accordingly so everything will work out for the best.

When something seemingly bad happens in your life, keep in mind that usually the only thing that changes is your mental state. The world is still a wonderful place to live in, you still have friends and family who love you, flowers are still beautiful and fragrant, the sun still shines, and vibrant life goes on.

There always will be bumps in the road, mostly small ones, and once in a while a bigger one. These are natural, and we all experience them. It is essential to be proactive in order to reduce the number of bumps and overcome the ones you do experience by learning and realigning.

Of course, some lessons won't be understood as easily or quickly and are meant to be slowly absorbed and pondered upon before they can fully be understood.

Almost everything happens for a good reason, and it's up to you to find out that reason. Remember, sometimes the reasons become clear quickly while other times the reasons take days, months, or even years to fully understand. As long as you are a good and positive person, you can be confident that good and positive results will come about even from seemingly bad situations.

I can think back to a few seemingly bad situations that I am now very grateful to have experienced. For example, when I was in my late twenties, I broke off a relationship that most likely would have redirected my life and put me in a situation in which I would not want to be. Another time, I didn't apply on time to a top university and decided to get my master's degree at a very good university instead. Because I did not go to the top university, I was able to focus more energy on creating my own businesses instead of planning my future based on graduating from the top college and becoming a financial analyst for a corporation.

If those seemingly bad situations had not happened, my life would be completely different, and I probably would not have written this book.

Everything happens for a good reason. It's up to you to find out why.

Extract the Good from the Bad

Failures are lessons that guide us toward success.

When something "bad" happens to you, it is usually something nudging you to get back on track and headed in the right direction.

Once you have analyzed the situation thoroughly, start to use that information to your benefit. See it as a lesson to learn from or a warning that you shouldn't be flowing in that direction.

Learning from each bad situation is the key to improving and becoming even better than you were before.

Sometimes you will be stuck in a seemingly bad situation until you learn your lesson. Once you have learned what that circumstance has to teach you, your eyes will open, and you will see the path to overcoming it.

In order to extract the good from the bad, you have to admit that something went wrong. Then analyze the situation and learn from it. Use it to your advantage, know how to avoid it in the future, and see what new doors opened for you.

Look for the truth and the lesson within the negative situation to help you improve your current situation. You can extract some good from the majority of problems. It's up to you to analyze and figure out what the positive feedback is.

Many years ago, I was deeply in love with a girlfriend that I'd dated for about two years. All was going well with our relationship until her parents convinced her to go study for a year in Europe. I was in shock. How could she go to Europe for a year, especially having heard that long-distance relationships were very difficult to maintain? I told her a million reasons why she shouldn't go, but she left anyway. We continued to be boyfriend and girlfriend, but after a few weeks, I heard negative rumors about her that I didn't enjoy, so I broke it off.

I soon found out the rumors weren't true, regretted what I had done, and tried to get back together with her. It was too late: she had found somebody else, and my heart was shattered into a thousand pieces.

It was a couple of years before I was able to overcome that situation and clearly see the huge benefits that came from our breakup. The bad results were easy to see: My emotions were in the floor, and I was extremely sad. I couldn't see the positive things in my life because I was focusing on the negative. Significant aspects of my life lost their importance, and nothing seemed to matter anymore. I felt very alone and my plans for the future were quickly altered.

The situation was a warning that my life was heading in the wrong direction. After I had learned and realigned my life, it put me back on track.

With time I extracted great results from that bad experience:
- I continued to be an independent entrepreneur instead of possibly joining her family's business and working in the insurance industry.
- I was able to travel frequently without any commitments back home. This opened the doors to new business ventures, long-lasting friendships, and more learning experiences, which helped me and my writing.
- Many years later I met and married a woman who was more aligned with me. We had many important values in common that

- held our relationship strong, and she would eventually become the perfect mother for my children.
- I gained a few more years of being single during which I experienced many life-enhancing events that taught me a great deal and helped me head toward a direction that would allow me to help people with my coaching and writing.
- I started to write this book after hitting rock bottom emotionally, financially, and physically.
- I experienced intense feelings of sadness and sorrow, which would later help me understand other people who had been through similar experiences and allow me to better help them.

Analyze what good comes out of seemingly bad situations. The lessons they offer can be life-enhancing steps that bring you closer to obtaining your true desires.

Aligned Action

One action is worth more than a thousand words.

More important than what you learn from this book is what you do with that knowledge. Applying the knowledge by taking action is the master key to the Positive Attraction System.

Thoughts by themselves are not nearly as powerful as thoughts paired with action. It is necessary that both your thoughts and your actions be aligned with what you desire. When you align your thoughts with your actions, you align the mental with the physical, the intangible with the tangible.

Your thoughts are not aligned with your actions when you think of doing something but end up doing something else or nothing at all. If you want to be successful at something, but instead of learning and practicing, you spend all of your free time distracted with unimportant activities, it will be very difficult for you to succeed. You must think about what you want and then follow through with aligned action.

For example, when people think about being healthy and trim but keep eating junk food, their actions contradict their thoughts. Instead, they should take action and select healthy, natural foods to eat, not simply think about doing so. Your actions must be aligned with your thoughts and desires in order for Positive Attraction to work to its fullest extent.

Without aligned actions, even highly focused thoughts and feelings rarely become reality.

I have met very intelligent people who knew exactly what to do to improve their situations and make their desires become reality. They were knowledgeable people who had studied and learned what to do to improve their lives. But their major flaw was a very basic one: they didn't apply that knowledge.

Such individuals keep complaining and even repeating to themselves what they need to do in order to achieve what they desire, but they don't take action. This keeps them in the same place, guaranteed. Years pass, and they still have the same issues and desires. They know what they need to do to achieve their desires, but they will not succeed until they move forward with that knowledge.

The door is open; all they have to do is step through.

Positive results don't just happen by themselves. You have to make them happen by taking action.

If I had not taken action to write this book, it simply wouldn't exist today, and you would not be reading it right now. My thoughts and feelings by themselves didn't magically create a book and place it in your hands. I had to create it.

Just thinking, adding feelings, and visualizing myself being a successful author wouldn't have done much unless I took that action. While learning more about my subject, about other successful authors, and about how to publish a book, I started to write, and I gained additional valuable knowledge by helping people through my coaching practice.

I aligned my thoughts with my actions and achieved what I desired.

Write Down Your Desires Today!

There is a big difference between thinking of something and writing it down. Writing it down is taking action, and as we've seen before, it should be one of the first steps toward making it happen.

By writing down what you want, you are taking action, relaying your thoughts, and creating something by using your hands (to write or type). This action not only creates something that didn't exist before (visible text), but it also reaffirms the idea and programs it into your subconscious. The process of clarifying your desire, refining it, and molding it in your mind occurs both before and during the time you write it down.

After you record your desires, add to each one by writing down the possible ways to attain it. You now have something physical to look at. You can also have something to listen to when you read it out loud.

Five actions—not just two—actually take place when you write down your desire and read it out loud: you *think* about your desire, you *write* about it, you *see* it on paper (or a screen), you *read* it out loud, and you *listen* to yourself reading it out loud.

When you take action by writing it down, you are telling your conscious and subconscious minds how much you want that desire, and both will respond accordingly. I have found that when I write down what I want, my desires become reality much faster than when I only think about them.

Saturate yourself with what you want. Make it a part of you. Say it out loud, write it down, and talk about it. Convert the thoughts about your desires into something tangible in order to give them more power and accelerate the process of bringing them into your reality.

A Key to Success: Keep Moving Forward

Success loves motion.

An important part of being successful is to keep moving forward by doing your day-to-day activities while at the same time taking new actions that can improve your life and help you reach your desires.

When you are moving forward, you are creating momentum and are in control. It's much harder to receive a new opportunity when you're standing still. You need to keep moving forward and never give up. Movement will eventually bring an opportunity that will be just what you are looking for, one that will guide you in the right direction to improve your situation and reach your desires.

Even when something negative happens in your life, you have to keep moving forward to maintain your momentum. It is much easier to keep moving forward than it is to stop and then start again.

If you're at a standstill, your situation may change very slowly, and most of the time not at all.

Yes, you periodically may slow down to think things over, but never completely stop for long periods of time. Keep living your life. Movement will help you to get over your issues and reach your desires much faster.

What Should I Do When I Am Feeling Sad and Down?

Our greatest glory is not in never failing,
but in rising up every time we fail.

—Ralph Waldo Emerson

If you are feeling down, then stand up, start learning, start communicating, start socializing with positive people, and start moving forward.

Movement will open doors and help you overcome issues.

Figure C-2: Issues Shouldn't Make You Stop Moving

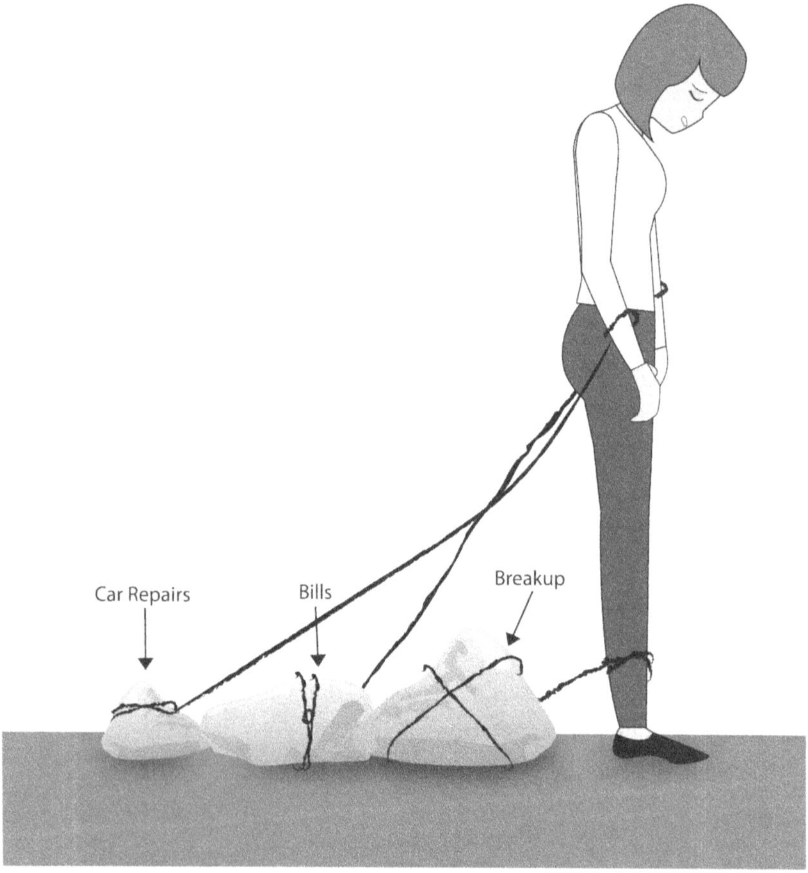

No matter how bad or down you might feel, everything changes sooner or later. You will feel better, you will feel positive again, and you will receive what you want. It's all about persistence. Never give up; always keep moving forward. The key word in the previous sentence is *moving*. Taking action is one of the most effective ways to change and improve situations in your life.

If you hide and cross your fingers, hoping your situation will magically change, it most likely won't. When you stop moving, you hand control of your life over to your outside world. It's you who needs to make things change and improve.

Even if you start moving in the wrong direction, you will eventually figure it out and realign toward the right one. The only way to improve your current situation is to keep moving forward.

If you feel down and it seems like the whole world is against you, remember that it's not. The world did not change from one day to the next and all of a sudden start to cause problems for you. The world is the same as it was yesterday. It is the same as it was when you were feeling happy.

Here is something I wrote when I felt down-and-out:

Every night has a dawn. The sun will always shine again tomorrow; darkness is temporary and controllable. Look ahead, the light is waiting for you. Start moving forward.

The past is over and done. It's all about what you are doing now and will do tomorrow.

Every positive action has a positive reaction, always.

If you are always getting the same results from the actions you take, and the results are not what you want, then you should do things differently. Change your approach, and you will have different results. Keep changing the way you do things until you get the result you want.

Figure C-3: Continued Movement Sometimes Requires More Effort but Always Brings Great Results

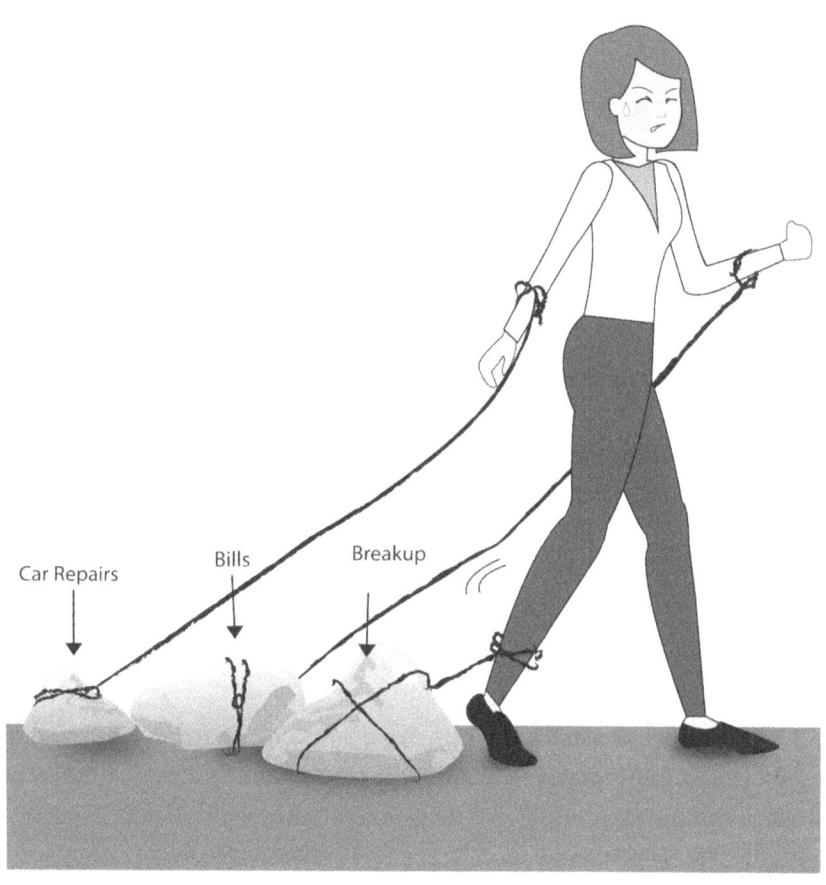

I have experienced a few highly negative and very difficult situations that lasted for long periods of time. Now that I look back, I can clearly see that in the initial years when I was feeling down, my life was on a downward spiral because I had stopped taking actions that could improve my situation.

After years of the same problems, the main reason my life began to improve was that I started to move.

POSITIVE ATTRACTION STEP #3: TAKE ACTION!

Figure C-4: Keep Moving Forward to Improve Your Situation

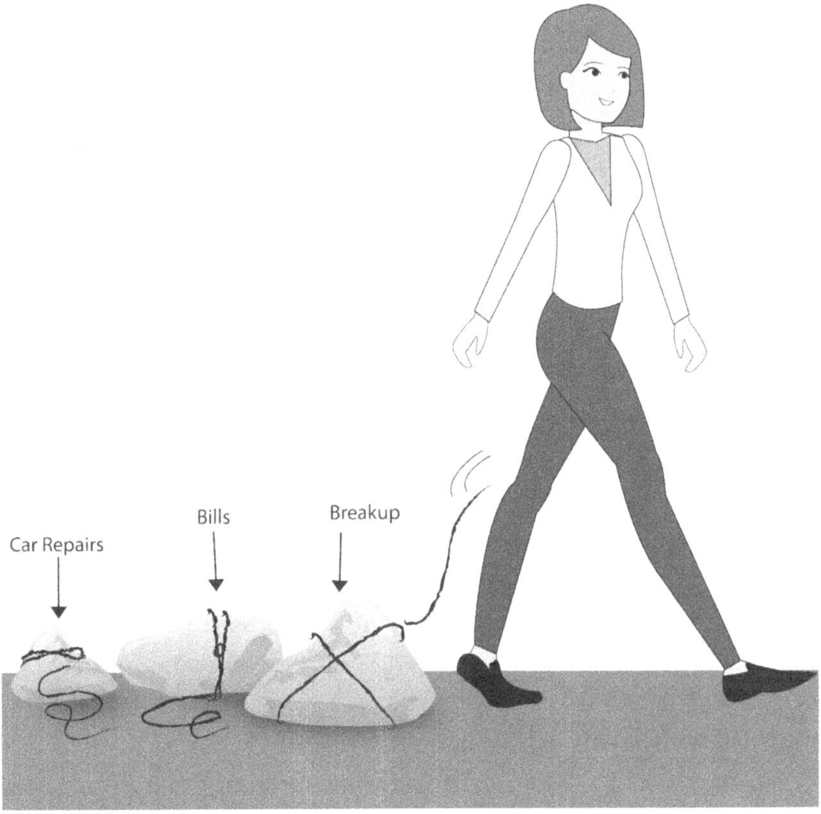

Once I started to move, to act and think like the positive person I had been before (and still was, deep down inside), everything started to change for the better.

Take control of your life by moving and realigning your actions with your desires today!

Keep an Open-Door Policy

When one door of happiness closes, another opens; but often we look so long at the closed door that we do not see the one which has been opened for us.

—Helen Keller

Opportunities will arrive to guide you in the direction in which you want to go. You need to choose the correct options from the ones presented to you and take action in order to benefit from them. You don't know when an opportunity will come, so keep your eyes open and follow through when you see hints or openings.

When you want something, a door will be opened for you. All you have to do is take action and walk in. You are getting the opportunity that you have been asking for—now move forward, and walk through the door. Once you walk inside, you simply need to keep moving forward until you reach your goal.

You have to look in order to find.

Take advantage of good opportunities immediately. If an opportunity is guiding you in the correct direction, keep taking action and moving forward in order to get closer to what you want.

Don't hesitate. If you see an opening, go through it. That's one of the most important parts of the Positive Attraction System: when you see an opportunity to get what you want, take action immediately to start making it a reality.

Notice that sometimes when we receive an opportunity, our minds can play tricks on us, saying, "That's too easy. It can't be real," or "What if I take it and it's not what I want?" The only way to find out is to watch for opportunities and follow through with them.

You have to keep your eyes and mind open in order to clearly see the opportunities that become available.

Watch for Opportunities in Disguise

Some opportunities will come disguised as something else.

On occasions you will get a random opportunity that will seem like it doesn't apply to what you desire, but it might be exactly what you need.

An opportunity may come disguised as a recommended book, an invitation to a party, a conference, lunch with friends, being introduced to someone, asked to help in a new activity, and so on.

Give it a chance: follow through and find out what it has to offer.

The right opportunity might come from an unexpected source and at first sight might not seem to contain what you want. That opportunity, though, might lead you to your goal through different means.

Keep in mind that the opportunities you take must be positive. They should never be opportunities that will affect you or others in a negative way. In other words, if you are offered to do something that is unethical or something that is obviously not positive, don't follow through with it. The majority of opportunities in life *are good* and should be followed through, just use common sense.

Opportunities help you achieve your goals. Keep an open mind, be flexible and follow through.

Even though some opportunities will take you out of your comfort zone, they will bring the change that is needed in your life for you to learn, grow, and head toward the direction that leads to your desire. Positive opportunities, no matter how unrelated they might seem to your desire, will always be beneficial to you and should be received with open arms.

When your door is closed, you are shutting the world out and effectively blocking yourself from being led toward your desires.

Figure C-5: Closed Door Shuts Out New Opportunities

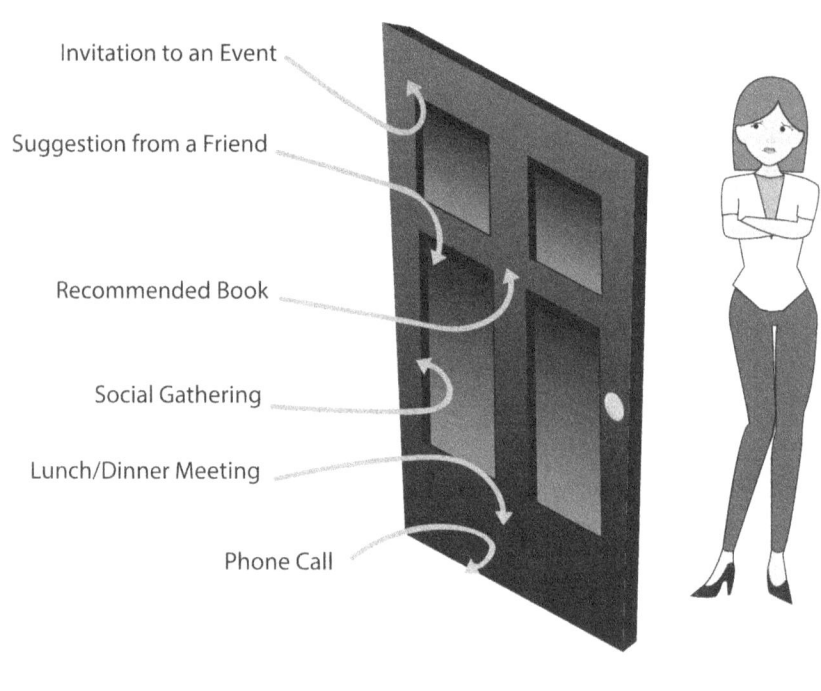

Keep your door open in order to let new opportunities come in and allow them to help you reach your desires.

If you really want to attain what you desire, you must take action. The new actions will take you in a different direction. Put in the extra effort, take different and better actions, and you will get different and better results.

When you see openings for opportunities, make sure that you act on them immediately.

If you don't feel like following through because you're tired, not sure if it will work, too busy, unwilling to change your daily routine, and so on, you need to admit to yourself that those are not valid reasons. In order to reach your desires, you need to adapt to the new directions they will lead you toward.

POSITIVE ATTRACTION *STEP #3: TAKE ACTION!*

Figure C-6: Open Door Allows New Opportunities to Come In and Help You Reach Your Desire

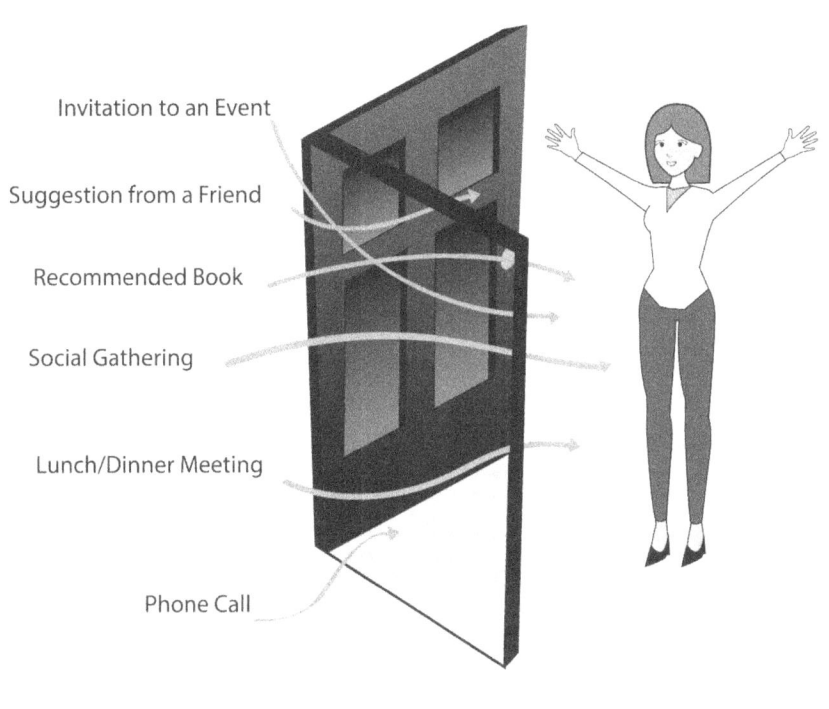

The direction you are currently heading in got you where you are now. Getting to where you want to be might require you to head in a different direction and try new opportunities.

Your results will be directly proportional to how much effort you put in. The more effort you put in, the more you will get out. The possibility of attaining your desires greatly increases when you accept that change is good. Once you've accepted this, you will be willing, able, and ready to follow through with an opportunity when it arises.

As you know by now, you have gotten where you are today from your past thoughts and actions. Your new and present thoughts and actions will get you where you want to be. You should be flexible and open-minded to do things you might not have done before. Start learning and absorbing new information that pertains to what you want.

105

Thomas, a client of mine, was down on his luck. His recent attempts at launching businesses had been very time-consuming and capital-intensive, and all ended up failing. He was deeply in debt and had to figure out how to support his wife and two young daughters.

On his last attempt at starting a business, he not only ended up closing it and losing money again, but, having invested in real estate with partners whom he later found out weren't very ethical, he also faced a costly legal battle.

His stress level was extremely high. His overwhelming and increasing debt created major issues in his personal life, friction with his wife, health issues, and overall feelings of helplessness and sadness.

This situation continued for several years. Eventually he had to ask a family member to loan him money. He asked for just enough to cover a few months of expenses so that he could pay for his children's school, food, rent, and the essentials.

One day he decided he needed professional assistance and came to me for help. After a few weeks of coaching him and teaching him the Positive Attraction System, I pointed out that one of his major flaws was that he had his doors closed to any and all opportunities that came his way.

With the new knowledge and mind-set he acquired, he was determined to change his actions and accept those opportunities.

Shortly after, a friend invited him to a dinner party.

Even though he was feeling down that day, still engulfed in a situation with no apparent way out, and really not in the mood for a social gathering, he agreed to go.

At the party, he happened to meet a person with a very good product to sell. Thanks to his past "failed" businesses, Thomas had learned an extensive amount about product distribution.

The two agreed to work together to try to get the product on the market. A large company gave them a chance, agreeing to start with one small batch for a three-month trial period. If the product passed the test, the company would consider ordering more.

The product was of such good quality that within one week the customer went from buying enough for one store to ordering for three more stores. The following week Thomas received an order for thirty-two more stores. The company's interest and Thomas's hard work kept improving the customer relationship. Within a few short months, the company ended up buying the product for all five hundred of its stores.

Thomas had faith that he could overcome his obstacles, gained the knowledge of how to do so, and took action. The gut-wrenching situation he'd struggled with for years changed over the course of just a couple of months.

This transformation, from a life full of negative events to a life full of positive ones, was possible because he followed through with an opportunity that didn't seem very promising—a simple dinner party. Yet the benefits it led him to changed his life.

Notice that even if Thomas had kept his doors closed, the invitation to the dinner party still would have been offered. But had he not accepted and followed through with it, he would have missed out completely.

Great opportunities are constantly coming to you. Give them a chance, keep your eyes and doors open to let them in, and follow through to find out what they have to offer.

Stop! Look Where You Are Heading

Sometimes we think we are heading the right way, but our actions are actually pointing us in the opposite direction.

As you can see in the figure below, the person is driving straight, and the car is moving in a straight line. However, his goal might not be in the direction in which he is heading. The driver's goal is actually in a different direction, to his left in this example. As he drives, he looks at and focuses on his left, and he thinks he is heading toward the goal he's looking at. But his actions are actually leading him down the wrong path.

Figure C-7: Thoughts and Actions Need to Head in the Same Direction

It might be obvious for someone on the outside to notice this and tell him, "Hey, you're heading in the wrong direction! You're heading toward a rough path if you keep going down that road." Yet stubbornly the driver thinks he's heading in the correct direction because his mind is focused on his desire. He is ignoring the fact that his actions are actually directing him the wrong way.

If you think you are heading in a positive direction but you're experiencing many negative results, your life will not improve and may even worsen unless you change. Don't ignore the warnings on the problematic road; recognize them and correct your direction instead.

Stop and take a look at yourself and your surroundings. If you notice that you or your surroundings or both are worsening, then realign and correct your direction so you don't end up in a place that is far from where you wanted to be.

It's always good to have a positive mental attitude and think that you are heading in the right direction, but it's also important to be honest with yourself. Acknowledge and accept your reality when you are heading in the wrong direction in order to realign and head in a positive one.

Actions always should be aligned with thoughts.

How Do You Know When You Are Heading in the Right Direction?

It's important to be honest with yourself about the results you obtain when you make changes. You can't improve your situation when you superficially think you are already heading in the right direction even though in reality you are not.

An effective way to measure how you are doing is to notice whether you are generating good or bad emotions while heading in your current direction. Also, write down the positive and negative events that have taken place since you started to head toward your goal.

Are you getting closer to it or further from it? Do the results give you energy and make you feel happier, or are they depleting your energy and making you feel down?

It's important to stop once in a while, look at your current situation, and then acknowledge your progress. If you are getting further from your goal, then adjust your approach. Repeat this process as needed until you start heading in the right direction.

When your situation keeps getting better and better, progress seems almost effortless, and the timing is perfect, those are good signs that you are heading in the right direction.

On the other hand, if you make a change that causes a big issue or takes you off track, it might be a bump in the road letting you know that you need to realign.

The closer attention you pay to changes in your life, the actions you are taking, and the resultant reactions, the easier it will be for you to correct yourself and stay on the right track.

There are signs that notify you when you are heading in the right direction: you will feel positive energy running through your body, you'll be happy and energetic, you'll experience less stress, and you will have a more positive attitude. Everything will start to fall into place smoothly.

The more positive your direction is, the happier you will be.

Be Truthful to the Most Important Person: You

It is important to be honest with yourself about your current situation. There is no need to hide the truth because you are the creator of your reality. You need to analyze your situation correctly in order to improve it.

The more honest you are with yourself, the more you can improve your situation. Only you know the full truth about yourself. Be honest.

It is very difficult for people to improve their reality when they are in denial and think they are already doing well. Real positive changes will come only when they accept their reality.

For example, someone might think she is happy, outgoing, and an overall positive person. But the reality is that all she talks about are negative events in her life. She rejects any possible life-improving opportunities offered to her, criticizes people, and even disrespects her loved ones by insulting them.

Until she accepts the reality that her life in general is overflowing with negativity, it will be very difficult for her to change. Accepting her current situation will be a major step toward her improvement.

Life's Predictable Ups and Downs: Good and Bad Rolls

Like many things in nature, our lives are cyclical. Just as a warm season is followed by a cold season, we also have good and bad rolls.

There is such a thing as being on a roll. When an athlete is on a roll, he or she is winning most of the time. There is such a thing as being on a bad roll, too, and if the athlete is rolling negatively and continues without changing, he or she will continue to lose.

It is normal and natural to have both good rolls and bad rolls. Just like the seasons, your highs and lows will come and go. It's up to you to take advantage of the highs and be prepared for the lows.

Good Rolls

Being on a roll is a sign that you are flowing in the right direction. Everything seems to fall perfectly into place. Everything you do and everyone you are in contact with respond just the way you planned. Most of the time, in fact, the responses are even better than expected. Take advantage of this situation because this is when you can do things faster, more efficiently, and with the best results.

A good roll could last only a few hours, days, weeks, or months. Sometimes a good roll will last for years, but sooner or later it will end, which is also part of the cycle.

Bad Rolls

When you see that you are on a bad roll, stop. Don't persist in making things happen by forcing them.

Each time something negative happens, it decreases your positive energy, makes you weaker, and opens up the possibility to attract more negative events. Just as positive attracts positive, negative attracts negative. When you accumulate a number of negative results from previous bad rolls, the likelihood of rolling bad again is increased.

Once in a while, something will happen that you didn't want or expect. This does not necessarily mean you are on a bad roll. It is part of life to have occasional disappointments. But when many bad things happen in a row and you can feel the negativity building up, that is when you are on a bad roll.

Sometimes when playing a game, and in life, you might start to experience constant negative results, and no matter what you do, nothing works out. This is a signal to stop and adjust. You lose the most when you don't acknowledge that you are on a bad roll and continue to play before getting rid of the bad vibes.

A bad roll can last as long as you continue doing the same actions without any adjustment. In some circumstances, it is mostly a state of mind. If you let it affect you, it will; if you don't, it won't. It's mostly about how you think and feel, so let the causes of the negative vibes slide right off you.

Imagine yourself being protected by a strong coat of positive energy so that anything unwanted bounces right off. You can be practically immune to negative energies. Anytime you notice that the negative energies are not being blocked as effectively as you think they should be, add stronger positive protection to your mind and feelings.

To benefit the most from this information, it is essential to take advantage of the good rolls in your life and recognize, acknowledge, and stop the bad rolls as soon as possible.

When on a good roll in life, accumulate the gains from your positive outcomes (i.e., save money, increase your health, strengthen your relationships) in order to be prepared for the bad rolls and lessen their possible negative effects.

Always Invest in Yourself

When you invest as much as you can afford in yourself, you will reach your goals faster. You will be happier, healthier, richer, more intelligent, and more fulfilled in your relationships.

Some ways to invest in yourself include the following:
- Buy books, videos, and audio recordings that will teach you more about what you desire.
- If you need to sleep better, buy blackout curtains, an eye mask, earplugs, or whatever helps you sleep better and be more rested. With more sleep, your mind will be sharper, you will be more energized, you will look and feel younger, and you will be more productive.
- If you have a choice between a monthly gym membership and a monthly payment on a new TV, choose the gym. The new TV will benefit you as much as the old one, and it won't improve your life. Doing exercise will.
- Invest the extra dollar or two in a healthier meal; your body and mind are worth it. Natural food, though it may be more expensive, will provide clean fuel to increase your energy and maintain your health.

The more you invest in yourself, the more you will grow as a person and the healthier, wiser, and wealthier you will be. Every penny that you invest to expand your knowledge and well-being will pay off many times over in all areas of your life.

Why You Need a Virtual (or Real) Coach

Coach is a simple word, yet it describes a very special type of person. A coach is a giving person who helps others through specialized teachings.

We are surrounded by coaches. There are all types of them. When we were young, we followed our parents' instructions. They coached us to be what they believed to be good, and this is why some of us turned out to be very similar to our parents. When you learn from somebody, whether that person considers himself (or herself) a coach or not, that person is coaching you. Often we serve as coaches to others, as well.

There are many different levels and types of coaching, and you can learn from anyone who is already doing what you want to do. You can analyze, learn, and implement what you like about successful people.

To get to where you want to be, start learning from the experts. An expert should specialize in areas you need improvement in and be someone who can help you attain your goal. Learn more about experts and leaders you admire and want to emulate.

If, for example, you want to lose weight, then start learning from people who are successful in losing weight. If you want to improve your relationship, see what people with happy relationships are doing.

You don't have to wait days or weeks to find someone to learn from or to coach you. You can start with one coach today and get another one down the road if need be. The important thing is to start with at least one as soon as possible.

Easily Accessible Professional Coaches

Coaches don't have to be people to whom you are already close. You don't have to know someone personally in order to learn from him or her. You can learn from proven coaches by reading their books, listening to their audio recordings, watching their videos, and so on.

Nowadays you don't even have to spend a dime to start. Thanks to the Internet, you can instantly follow and learn from coaches, many of whom have their own websites and blogs or are available on social networking sites. The information they make available to the general public is usually free to access.

I highly recommend that you find at least one person to choose as a coach. Coaches should have two or more of the following prerequisites:
- They have positively improved their own lives with what they do.
- You admire them. (This can come later if the coach is new to you.)
- They motivate you to become a better person.
- They have reached or surpassed a similar desire to yours and now teach other people how to do it.
- They are top experts in the field that interests you.
- They have published a book on the area you want to improve in.

You can conduct a search on the Internet or in a bookstore to find experts in any given field. Find a good website or book on the topic that interests you, learn from it, and find out more about the author to see what other tools for learning he or she offers.

The most successful coaches are published authors and experts in their fields. Just reading, seeing, and listening to what these experts have to say will start to change the way you think and motivate you to reach your desires faster.

You can find a professional coach for any topic that interests you. Start today by visiting a coach's website, reading his or her books, watching his or her videos, or listening to his or her audio recordings. Invest in yourself, and it will pay back hundreds of times in more ways than you can imagine.

Should I Force Things to Happen or Let Them Happen Naturally?

The best way to make things happen is to let them unfold naturally, with very little force.

The more you force things, the harder it will be to reach your goals. In situations that require some amount of pressure to get what you want, apply only enough pressure to keep yourself moving forward. Very few situations should require large amounts of force.

The more relaxed you are and the more confidently you do things, the better the results will be. The more relaxed your mind is, the more accurate your decisions will be.

We have all experienced situations in which we tried to force something to happen, and because of that forcing, we actually prevented it from happening. If you think back to that situation, you'll notice that without so much force, the outcome might have been better.

Situations in our lives are similar to branches. Most of the time, you can bend a branch with a small amount of force, and nothing negative will happen to it. But if you apply too much force when bending the branch, it will either crack or completely break. Instead of gently guiding the situation along, the excess force destroyed it.

It's important to learn to analyze circumstances to know when to guide a situation gently and when to apply some force. About 80 percent of situations should be guided gently; only 20 percent of the time will they require higher degrees of force.

Be persistent in getting what you want, but don't overdo it.

Every Single Event in Your Life Is a Reaction to a Previous Action

Nothing just happens in life; actions cause things to happen.

It's important to be able to distinguish between actions and reactions, causes and effects.

When an event occurs, a reaction is taking place. Something caused the event to occur. An action took place that caused that reaction. Some examples of reactions to previous actions include the following:

- When someone gets sick, it doesn't just happen. Something changed in his or her body (action) and caused that illness (reaction).
- When you learn more about what you like to do (action) and an opportunity comes along, your knowledge and preparedness allow you to take the opportunity (reaction) and be successful.
- When you say positive and uplifting words to someone (action), you build that person's confidence, make his or her star shine brighter, and add happiness to his or her life (reactions).
- The healthier the food you eat (action), the healthier your body becomes (reaction).
- The happier you become (action), the more successful you will be (reaction).

If you want to improve a situation in your life, look at its real cause. Trace the effect back to the root of the problem, step by step.

Once you determine the cause, you can adjust accordingly. When you change the actions, those changes will also alter the reactions.

Everything Counts in Large Amounts

Even if you do a little bit each day, one thing is for sure: time goes on. Before you know it, little things have added up, and big results have occurred. Whether it is walking an extra five minutes a day, eating one less bite of food when you are already full, smoking one less cigarette, or starting to kiss your loved one once a day, all these things have big effects after a while.

There is always room for improvement. You just need to keep moving in the right direction, even if your steps are small.

Before you know it, you will have reached your destination—you will obtain your desire.

I once had a client, named Jack, who went on a diet because he'd gained some weight. I asked him if he'd started going to the gym again. He said he didn't have time to commit to going three times a week, so he hadn't gone at all. When I told him to go one day a week instead, he looked at me with a startled expression. I said, "Sure, going one day out of the whole week is better than not going at all." He would be going four times a month, or fifty-two times a year. Not bad when you compare it to zero times.

The important thing is to start taking action, even if it's small. Not only does it all add up, but it's also a lot easier to grow than to start from zero.

Anything is always better than nothing.

When starting from zero, even small things add up. Here are some ideas:
- Health: Drink one less soda a week, drink a freshly made natural juice or eat a piece of fruit once a week, or park farther away or walk longer distances on purpose one day a week.
- Money: Try to save at least one percent of your income each month. You should also invest in a book that helps you become better at your work or the type of work you would like to be doing, to improve your skills and earn more money.
- Relationships: Say "I love you" once a week to a loved one, give a compliment to a loved one once a week, and say "thank you" once in a while for something routine that someone does for you.

Every small action has a large impact over time.

Once you start taking baby steps and become accustomed to them, you will notice the positive effects they make in your life, which will likely motivate you to take even bigger steps.

Remember that in life everything counts in large amounts.

When Not to Act Like You've Already Received Your Desire

Most of the time, for the Positive Attraction System to work at its fullest, you should act as if you've already attained your desire. The rest of the time, you should remain focused on your desire but divide it into parts to prevent skipping important natural steps.

For example, if you think a person you've just started to date will make a good husband or wife, it doesn't make sense to act as though you are already married to that person. If one day you are acting casually and the next as if he or she is your spouse, that might come as a shock to him or her. Such behavior might push the person away from you instead of bringing him or her closer, even if he or she was interested in you before.

Acting as if you've already attained your goal can also be detrimental to your progress if you start to slow down and get complacent about reaching your desire. Although you may be acting as if you have already reached your desire, you aren't there yet. You are only acting that way in order to align your thoughts and actions and make the process more effective. Don't let yourself slide into a comfort zone until you actually attain the goal.

Use common sense. In some situations, it will be best if you act as if you have already attained your desire, and in other cases it will be best if you focus on your final goal but take one step at a time in order to get there.

If you are in doubt and you feel it's hard to act as if you've already achieved your desire, then act as though what you desire is in progress. Divide it into several steps, and keep visualizing your final goal. Start molding yourself to it at your own pace, remembering that the best results come smoothly, naturally, and without force.

Every day you will be getting closer to it until it's yours.

You Are What You Do

If a man thinks saintly thoughts but his actions are devilish, how will he be viewed?

As a devilish person, of course.

You are what you do, not only what you think.

I once helped a woman who thought positive thoughts most of the time. She was an extremely positive person (the most positive-thinking person I have ever met, in fact) even though her life was highly stressful and full of problems. She worked long hours at a job she didn't like, raising her kids and catching up with her housework in the evenings and in her "free" time.

She wanted good things for herself and her loved ones, and she knew what direction to take, but she did nothing about it. Her major issue was that she only *thought* about how to improve her life. Her actions remained the same, and this kept her in the same place.

Once she took action, even though the actions were very small at first, she started a domino effect. She soon started to get positive results in her life, which started to guide her life in a better direction. She started to communicate more with her loved ones, and her situation started to improve.

This woman had been locked in an artificial, invisible, self-imposed cage. Her fears and feelings of helplessness kept her there. Even though she felt helpless, the truth was very different. She—like every single one of us—has the potential to do and become whatever she wants. All it took to start the chain of positive events that improved her life was a change of perception and the small spark of positive results created by her new actions.

Thinking is the spark; taking action is the fire.

My Favorite Five-Letter Word: *Learn*

I will prepare and some day my chance will come.

—Abraham Lincoln

You are what you know. That's what got you to where you are today. Now imagine that you knew more about what you do or would like to do. Where would that take you? Most likely it would take you somewhere better than where you are now. Now imagine that you learn something new every day of your life. That would mean that from the day you begin learning till the day you are physically gone, your life could improve every single day.

When you learn something new, that information can open up your eyes to something that you couldn't see before, and then everything can start to make perfect sense.

All the knowledge that you need in order to achieve your desires already exists. It is accessible and available to you. You can start obtaining it by simply taking action and finding the relevant information. Some of it will be available for free, some you will have to purchase, and some may come directly from your subconscious mind. Once you have learned the information, don't stop there. Continue to take action by applying that information, allowing it to help you obtain your desires.

Nowadays there are many different ways to learn, all of them good in their own ways. Some methods work better than others, depending on your preferences. Here are some of the basic approaches:

- Read more about what you desire.
- Watch videos about what you desire.
- Listen to audio books on the topic.
- Experience it by trial and error.

It's likely that a biography of a person you admire and wish to emulate already exists. Reading biographies and autobiographies is a great way to see how other people have succeeded. You will learn something beneficial, and it will motivate you to get where you want to be faster.

The more you learn about what you do or would like to do, the faster you will achieve it.

The more you learn and use that information to grow and achieve balance, the more you will be able to earn, live, enjoy, love, and relax.

Learn about the field you already work in, the field you would like to be working in, your hobbies, the things that make you happy, and anything else that interests you.

When reading books on self-improvement, always keep in mind that no book in the world can improve your life unless you apply what you've learned. Make sure to *apply* the knowledge you learn from this and other books to your life. Action is the key.

Positive Attraction
Step #4: Feel

Positive Attraction Step #4
Feel: Happiness Is the Key to Success

*Understand that all thoughts create—and the more
emotion that is present at the time that a thought is set in motion, the
faster the creation will be received.*

—Esther Hicks

You are the only person in the world who knows exactly how you feel. Feelings aren't visible and can't be touched, yet they are very real. Even though feelings are intangible, they can be extremely powerful when applied properly.

Practice attaching feelings to your desires. The more positive the feelings you attach to what you desire are, the faster you will reach it.

Your outside world will improve to the same degree your inner world does. In other words, improve your inner world by having positive thoughts and feelings, and your outside world will follow.

How much it will improve depends on how much you really want what you desire and what actions you take to achieve it. Attach feelings to all your desires, and envelop them with as many intense positive emotions as possible. When you add feelings to your thoughts, they will produce the actions that will direct your life.

The Happier You Are, the More Successful You Will Be

Success is not the key to happiness.
Happiness is the key to success.

—Albert Schweitzer

The happier you are, the faster and more smoothly you will attract all the positive things you desire to yourself. The sadder you are, the more effort you will need to put into bringing about your desires. Being in a state of happiness is normal. Being unhappy most of the time is neither normal nor healthy.

Happy and positive energy is contagious. A little bit always rubs off on everyone you interact with. That's why some people have a certain something that makes others want to be around them: their happiness attracts. On the other hand, negative people (often unknowingly) repel others.

Most of the time, your mind controls your emotions and moods.

You can change your mood depending on what you think. You can change a bad situation into a positive one just by seeing it from a different perspective and learning from it. Instead of allowing the situation to produce negative emotions, extract the good from it and allow it to give you positive feelings and energy. Learn from it and move on. Focus on the good things to come. What you think of now, you will live later.

Do whatever it takes to naturally feel happier: laugh, socialize with positive people, play a fun game, listen to music with positive lyrics and uplifting melodies, go for a walk outside, or do anything else that makes you feel good.

Your Inner Power

Ninety-nine percent of who you are is invisible and untouchable.

—Rhonda Byrne

Your greatest power comes from within. You can greatly improve your life as you know it by accessing and increasing your inner power.

Your inner power includes your subconscious mind, which plays an important part in improving your life because of its connection with the Universal Mind.

You are powerful, strong, in control, resilient, pure, and full of radiant positive energy.

Your Inner Power as a Shining Star

You are full of living energy that is always on and constantly attracting things into your life. In this way, you are like a glowing star. The happier and healthier you are, the brighter you glow. Likewise, the sadder and unhealthier you are, the dimmer your star becomes.

This interaction between your interior world and your physical world is another reason it's important to remain as healthy as possible. The healthier you are, the stronger your inner power will be, and the more you will attract your positive desires into your life.

You radiate energy, and other people can sense it. We often refer to these energies we sense as good vibes or bad vibes.

For easier understanding, imagine your body as a container that is filled with a set amount of energy. You may add either positive or negative energy, but it is always full of various combinations. The goal is to keep it filled with as much positive energy as possible so that when negative people or situations come along and try to pass their negativity on to you, the positive energy will serve as a barrier and repel them.

Whether your container consists primarily of positive energy or negative energy, the more dominant of the two will attract more of its kind. The more positive you are, the more you will shine. The events in your life will tend to be positive. The more negative you are, the dimmer you will be, and the more negative the events in your life will be.

You have the potential to shine as brightly as the brightest star in the sky. The whole universe is on your side, wanting you to flourish and grow into the great and happy person you know you can be.

Now ask yourself, is what you're doing today making you brighter or dimmer?

Why Does Your Star Get Dimmer?

Your star might dim for many reasons, including the following:
- a problematic relationship
- excessive consumption of unhealthy food
- excessive use of alcohol, cigarettes, or other mood-altering substances
- high levels of stress
- exposure to negative information, whether you are reading, listening, or watching
- lack of sleep
- interaction with negative people

When your star dims, it's like a balloon losing its air. Your body actually feels like that. When you receive negative information, your positive energy begins to leak out, causing you to slowly cave in on yourself. You can be vibrant and happy, but when you are inundated by negativity, you feel like you are losing all the positive air that fills you up.

If your star is dim due to negative emotions, ignore the negative feelings as much as possible so that you don't attract more of them. If you don't feel well for whatever reason and you haven't been able to make yourself feel better, then keep on with your daily routine as you usually would. Your emotional state will become neutral if you ignore the negative feelings.

Being emotionally neutral is much like putting your emotions on cruise control and going through your usual routine for as long as it takes until you can get rid of your negative emotions and start attracting desirable things into your life again.

Being in a neutral state is preferable to feeling pessimistic and attracting more negativity into your life.

How to Make Your Star Shine Brighter

The following are some simple actions that will raise your positive energy level and make your star shine brighter:
- Focus on the good things in your life.
- Exercise (even if it's for a few minutes a week, everything counts in large amounts).
- Laugh.
- Listen to music that raises your energy level.
- Talk to positive friends and family. Whenever possible, visit them in person.
- Get a good night's sleep. Whenever possible, take a nap to help your body regenerate.
- Take a couple of showers each day in order to balance yourself, wash the bad vibes away, and bring in the good ones.
- Play a game or do something you enjoy.
- Take a relaxing walk. Leave your office or house for a few minutes, and change your surroundings.
- Keep moving. Don't slow down or let a negative situation pull you down. Keep doing your day-to-day activities, just as you did before the problem occurred.
- Compliment somebody about anything (nice smile, pretty earrings, cool watch, nicely done, I like your haircut, you're a great listener, and so on).
- Smile.
- Thank people for anything and everything they do for you. This includes waiters, coworkers, family members, and significant others.

The more often you do things that raise your positive energy level, the brighter your inner star will shine, and the happier you will be.

The Wonders of Sleeping Well

As we have just seen, sleeping well is one ingredient that makes your star shine brighter.

Let your body rest. Sleep well, and when tired, take a nap if possible. If your body isn't rested and well balanced, it's much harder to feel optimistic and attract positive energy.

Sleeping is as essential as eating and breathing. We already know that the better we eat, the better we feel and the healthier our bodies will be. This applies to sleeping as well.

Some benefits of sleeping well include the following:
- enhanced mood
- improved memory
- increased life-span
- improved decision-making ability
- lower levels of stress and anxiety
- greater emotional stability
- improved appearance
- improved concentration
- improved metabolism

The better you sleep, the more your body and cells recuperate and regenerate. You will also be more energetic, look better, feel younger, have a brighter inner star, and more quickly and efficiently attract your desires into reality.

Why Exercise Brings Your Desires Faster

The healthier you are, the more your star shines, and the happier you are. Exercise releases natural mood enhancers called endorphins.

I love to exercise. I see it as a way to escape my day-to-day routine and have some time to let go and treat myself to some fun.

I find exercise to be the best way to relieve all the pressure and stress that naturally builds up. It brings my mind and body back to equilibrium and naturally elevates my outlook on life.

Some of the benefits of exercise include the following:
- improved mood and psychological well-being
- easier weight control
- improved health conditions and lowered risk of diseases
- increased energy level
- improved sex life
- more youthful appearance and increased physical well-being
- improved memory and sleep
- improved bone strength, balance, and flexibility

After exercising, your mind is relaxed. You've released toxins and increased your positive energy level, and you look and feel great.

Remember that your mind is part of your body, so the healthier your body is, the healthier your mind is, and the more clearly it can think.

Exercising leads to a healthy body and creates positive thoughts and energy, all of which helps in attracting what you desire.

Laughing and Smiling Brighten Up Your Inner Star

It was only a sunny smile, but it scattered the night
And little it cost in the giving;
Like morning light,
And made the day worth living.

Anonymous

There is a direct correlation between how much you laugh and smile and how happy you are. The more you laugh and smile, the happier you will be.

Laughing is fun. It brings out the best in you and makes you feel vibrant and full of energy. It triggers the release of feel-good endorphins, decreases your stress level, and improves your health. Laughter is often referred to as the best medicine, and for good reason.

Do things that make you laugh: watch funny movies, hang around funny people, listen to or tell some jokes, play a game, kid around with somebody, watch comedians—in other words, have fun.

Laughter is usually caused by an outside factor, yet we can smile at any time and for any reason.

Smiling is contagious. When you see someone smiling at you, your natural reaction is to smile back. Having a smile on your face projects your level of positive energy to the world. When you smile, you radiate positive energy and will receive more positive energy in return.

There are many reasons to be happy and have a smile on your face. But even smiling for no particular reason at all will increase your positive energy level. Having a smile on your face is like turning on the switch for your positive energy.

Whenever you feel down, smile. Whenever you need an energy boost, smile. Whenever you are stressed, smile. For any reason or no reason at all, smile. Smiling improves your mood instantly and helps you see life more clearly and optimistically.

The more you smile and laugh, the greater the amount of positive energy you will give and receive. The more you give, the more you get.

Positive Music Enhances Your Mood

Music is one of the few natural and healthy sources of instant mood enhancement that I know of. Every time I play some of my favorite positive music, I get an immediate rush of positive energy.

Music that fills you with positive feelings can elevate your emotional state, reduce your stress level, raise your energy level, and energize your body and mind.

Create a playlist that lifts your spirits and makes you feel good. Everybody's tastes differ, so personalize your playlist to your liking.

Even though eighties music might be what creates positive feelings for me, someone else might prefer country music, pop music, easy listening, or even rock. Mix and match the music that makes you feel good, regardless of the differences in genre.

Remember that it doesn't matter what the genre might be; what matters is how the music makes you feel. Analyze the feelings that the music generates inside of you, group the positive songs accordingly, and listen to them often.

How Alcohol and Other Mood-Altering Substances Dim Your Star

The longer you are out of reality, the longer it will take for your reality to improve.

In order to reach your goals, you must control your life's direction. Abuse of mood-altering substances like alcohol and drugs can play a major role in preventing you from reaching your goals and being happy. Since feeling naturally positive is a very important part of the Positive Attraction System, try to avoid abusing mood-altering substances and intentionally placing yourself in a negative emotional state.

Alcohol can be enjoyable in moderation. When you drink too much, however, you begin to dehydrate your body (among other adverse side effects), and the following day you will probably have a hangover. Being hung over is obviously not a good feeling.

You can't focus on important things, or even normal things, when you are hung over. Since you are physically hurting on the inside, your mind is distracted and is not able to focus on anything else.

You can't continue to improve your positive flow when you are hung over. You can try to slow down and go with a neutral flow, which is OK to do in this type of situation, but most of the time you will flow negatively despite your efforts because your mind isn't capable of guiding you in the right direction.

Alcohol and drugs keep intelligent and potentially successful people from breaking past their comfort levels. When people abuse these substances, they are erecting barriers—self-imposed barriers—that limit their ability to improve their lives. Barriers created by consuming alcohol and other substances prevent you from taking control of your life.

Drinking too much dims your internal star and makes you lose sight of the direction in which you should be going. It is like pouring cold water on your star: it will smother and extinguish part of your inner power.

I noticed that when I was hung over, even though there might have been good things happening (as a result of my positive thoughts and actions from previous days), I wasn't able to enjoy them and be happy. Also, since I felt down, I started to think negatively and attract more negativity, magnifying my negative emotions tenfold.

Certainly, having one drink is fine. But just like everything else, excess is usually bad for your health and will dim your star.

You know what the end result of abusing mood-altering substances will be: feeling hung over, unresponsive, cranky, tired, and powerless. Try to use these substances infrequently, less often than you do now, or, if possible, not at all.

Celebrity Example

Take a look at celebrities. They might be very successful and living incredibly happy lives that many people would love to have. But when they start to overuse drugs and alcohol, their positive feelings start to dim, they lose connection to their inner guidance, and their lives begin to lose direction.

Abusing substances and alcohol creates a magnet that attracts bad feelings, which in turn brings bad decisions and bad results. Don't add more fuel to the problematic fire; turn it off instead.

Toxins Suffocate Your Cells—Cleanse and Detoxify Your Body

Your mind is part of your body. What affects your body has a direct effect on your mind.

If your body is unhealthy, your mind and thoughts may not be as healthy as they could be. The healthier your body is, the healthier your mind and thoughts can be.

It is important to know that almost everything you eat, drink, or breathe is absorbed by your cells and may become a permanent part of your body.

Some foods may taste good and be enjoyable for a few minutes while you eat them but make you feel bad shortly after. Food should make you feel good both while you eat it and after. If the food you eat is creating bad feelings inside of you, those negative emotions are effectively lowering your positive energy level and possibly slowing you down from reaching your desires.

It's always best to eat natural foods that make the body feel good because the better you feel, the more likely it is that you will reach your desires. Artificial and highly processed foods containing large amounts of chemicals and preservatives can make you feel bad, gain weight, and possibly fall ill. Eating and drinking processed foods suffocates your cells and inhibits your ability to thrive.

Your cells need natural vitamins and minerals in order to be healthy and productive. When the essentials they need are not available or are surrounded by toxic substances, cells become unhealthy. The toxins in your body start a chain reaction that starts to grow and affect your organs and other parts of your body.

Highly processed foods can cause highly processed illnesses.

Your cells want to breathe, but when they are surrounded by toxins, they begin to asphyxiate. The fewer toxins you ingest, the healthier your body will be and the longer and happier your life may be.

Everybody has directly or indirectly been exposed to toxins in foods, air, and water. These toxins accumulate in your body throughout your lifetime. One way to counteract this condition is to do a cleanse. This will help to detoxify your body in order for it to regain its healthy, clean, and natural state.

Cleansing your body not only removes the toxins, but it also may help your body to function at its fullest. Some of the documented benefits of cleansing are weight loss, improved sleep, skin clarity, immune system improvement, slowed aging process, and digestion regularity.

Think about your car for a moment. After a while, the motor oil and filter in the car need to be cleaned. Doing a cleanse is similar to changing the oil in your car. Different cleansing methods exist (i.e., oral administration, enemas, mineral baths, and so on), and by applying them, you can reset your body by eliminating the toxins that have accumulated, allowing it to be healthy and function at its fullest again.

Your mind and your body are all you are physically made of. Don't let a toxic environment and artificial, unhealthy foods bring you down. Detoxify and make your body clean, pure, and healthy again.

Always Think and Speak Positively about Yourself

*Positive words are like honey;
negative words are like poison.*

Always think and speak to yourself positively.

If at any time during your day you do something wrong or make a mistake, don't criticize yourself or put yourself down. Negative words are like poison.

I once had a client who was a very intelligent person, but he used to put himself down much of the time. He not only thought negatively when he made a mistake, but he also voiced his negative thoughts.

I could literally hear every time he thought he'd made a mistake. If it hadn't been for his verbal complaints, however, I wouldn't have known about these so-called mistakes.

When he tried to send me an e-mail but mistakenly typed the wrong letter in the address, he said out loud to himself, "That was stupid of me." When he forgot to pick up something at the grocery store, he said, "What an idiot I am for forgetting that." The list goes on.

This negative internal (or external) talk is actually pretty common. If this happens to you, instead of putting yourself down, either restrain yourself from saying anything or say something motivational like, "I will do it better next time," "I will be more careful," or "Every day I am learning and improving." Be creative as you try to replace your negative statements with positive ones.

I am my own best friend, mainly because I know every single thing about me. I know what I like, what I don't like, what makes me laugh, what makes me cry, and everything else in between.

Likewise, you are your best friend. Nobody knows you better than you do. Regardless of how other people and circumstances are affecting you, you should always be your own stable rock to lean on whenever you need to.

You need to motivate yourself, bring yourself up when you are feeling down, cheer yourself up, congratulate yourself, and always talk positively to yourself. This may sound a bit egocentric, but all you are doing is creating and growing the positive energy inside of you to make you a more positive, successful, and happy person. And the more positive you are, the more positive outcomes you will attain.

Your mind is the most powerful tool you have. Make sure you only say positive words to yourself. Practice filtering your thoughts and your inner dialogue, and allow them to fill you up with positive emotions.

Intensity of Emotions

When you add feelings to your thoughts, your heart speaks. When you speak from the heart, the universe listens.

An essential factor in the Positive Attraction System is the intensity of your feelings toward what you desire. You should learn to add as much positive feeling as possible to what you desire.

All of us are familiar with the experience of having a quick yet very intense and highly emotionalized sad thought—a thought so powerful it can immediately bring you to tears.

Highly emotionalized positive thoughts have the same amount of power. They can bring a smile to your face, make you feel energized, and make your star shine brighter.

For example, seeing a picture or a photograph of an incredibly beautiful, exotic place usually makes me want to be there. My desire to be there is so intense that just looking at the picture automatically raises my energy level. I instantly visualize the place, and the image in my mind and feelings of myself there pull me toward it while, at the same time, I attract it.

That's the type of feeling you should generate when you think about and visualize what you desire.

Feelings are powerful. The more you channel and control highly charged emotions to be positive, the happier you will be.

The more intense your emotions are toward what you desire, the more powerful your attraction will be, and the faster you will obtain it.

Your Precious Positive Minutes of the Day

The thirty minutes after you wake up and before you go to sleep are the most important minutes of the day. During this time you can more easily program your subconscious mind, making it the best time to surround yourself with positive thoughts and emotions. The following tips will help you to do so.

Follow these tips in the morning:
- Avoid checking your e-mail, chats, and social network accounts. Don't watch, read, or listen to the news or do anything that will distract you.
- While you still have a relaxed mind from waking up, review your desires. Visualize them, and live them in your mind.
- Repeat positive affirmations. You can personalize the following affirmation and use it when starting off the day: "Today is going to be a great day full of positive events. I am surrounded by powerful energies that make me stronger, more in control, and happier and always bring what's best for me." (More affirmations are available in the following section.)
- After finishing with the previous exercises, turn on some happy, motivational music, and enjoy your day.

Follow these tips before you go to bed at night:
- Just as in the morning, avoid doing anything that will distract you from your precious minutes to absorb positive thoughts.
- Get in a comfortable place (e.g., your bed or the sofa), and relax.
- Review your goals and desires.
- Repeat your positive affirmations.
- Visualize your desires, and think of how good you are going to feel when you reach them.

Try to make your thirty positive power minutes as pleasurable as possible. This is your time to relax and enjoy yourself. Visualize your desires as realistically as possible, and imagine how good it feels to reach them.

The routine you do during this time should be fun and enjoyable. It should not feel like homework. If it ever does, you should still do the process at least once, either in the morning or at night. Even doing it just once a day will gradually program your thoughts into your subconscious mind.

If you apply this process for three to four weeks, it will become a habit and flow smoothly and naturally: it will become part of your daily routine. Not only that, but it will help you get to your desires much faster.

Your Truths: Affirmations That Become Reality

*I focus upon the desires that I want to
see manifested in my life.*

Affirmations are fantastic. They are phrases made up of very powerful words that describe what you want. I like to call my affirmations my truths.

I call them my truths because the phrases describe what I truly want to be, what I know I can be, what I know I'm becoming, and what I know I am. Affirmations start off describing what you want to be, but very quickly they can become what you are.

Here is one of my favorite affirmations: *I am whole, perfect, strong, powerful, pure, healthy, young, confident, wealthy, successful, rich, intelligent, cool, harmonious, giving, loving, and happy.*

Another very effective method of using affirmations is to write them in the form of descriptive stories of how you want your life to be. The more descriptive and detailed they are, the more personalized and meaningful they become, and the more powerful and effective the results will be.

I used the following affirmation to attract the best woman for me: *My ideal woman is coming to me and is getting closer and closer to me every day. She is smart and beautiful, has a very nice body, is happy, athletic, giving, at peace with herself and her world, easygoing, feminine, and loving. Every day we are getting closer to each other. Soon we will be happily together for the rest of our lives.*

Adapt and mold your truths to your current desires. When you have become or received what you wanted, you can replace those words with new ones. The only time you shouldn't remove affirmations that represent fulfilled desires is when represent perpetual goals and should remain part of your regular affirmations (i.e., I am strong, healthy, loving, and so on).

To be as happy and balanced in your life as possible, make sure that your truths include words that pertain to areas in your life that need more improvement, including relationships, health, and wealth.

An effective way to start is by memorizing just three of your most important affirmations. Then add more every few days until you've memorized all of them. When creating your affirmations, make sure they are correctly associated and cause pleasure, not pain.

Incorrect: I don't want to be in debt.
Correct: I am financially free.

Incorrect: I don't want to be sick.
Correct: I am healthy.

When you state your affirmations, always believe they are true or attainable.

Whenever you have doubts or are feeling down, repeat your affirmations to yourself several times. As a minimum, repeat them in the morning when you wake up and before you go to sleep every night.

Saying your affirmations requires only a few seconds, but the improvements they bring into your life can last forever. Remember, you are reprogramming your subconscious mind by repeating your goals and affirmations to yourself. After a while, your subconscious mind will accept them as true, and you will begin to attract them into your life even faster.

When I use techniques that produce good results, I search for other ways to implement them. In regard to my affirmations, I not only have a long list of words and phrases that I read often, but I also purchased a good yet inexpensive smartphone app that reads back to me anything I type into it. Every morning when I wake up, or whenever I feel like it, I have the app play back all my affirmations.

If you don't have a smartphone, you can simply read out loud your affirmations and record them on any device with a microphone recorder so that you can play them back later. This is an easily accessible and effective practice that requires very little effort. Listening to your positive words and phrases when you wake up or before going to sleep (or when you are drowsy) stores them directly in your subconscious mind.

Just by pressing PLAY, you are effortlessly programming your subconscious with positive information about everything you want to bring into your life.

Good Affirmation Words to Use

Below are some sample affirmations, each followed by a list of words you can use to create your own personal affirmations. These words are a good place to start, but you can use any words that fit your needs.

Make a list of a few words you want to use so you can begin to repeat them to yourself today. You can always add more later—the important thing is to start now.

As the examples below show, they can be verbs, adjectives, nouns—anything that serves your purpose.

INCREASE HAPPINESS

Example: I am happy, optimistic, and surrounded by positive energies. I focus on the good things in my everyday life and in achieving my desires.

Words: joy, smile, laughter, cheerful, confident, courageous, sunny, bright, fun, family, fantastic, flowers, energetic, cheerful, delicious, delight, happy, humorous, optimistic, pleasure, giggle, rejoice

IMPROVE HEALTH

Example: I am healthy and strong, and I have clean and pure cells. I enjoy eating natural foods that are healthy. Every day I am improving my weight so I can look better, be healthier, and feel great.

Words: healthy, active, alive, pure, complete, perfect, clean, pure cells, athletic, blooming, firm, fit, flourishing, strong, good-looking, energetic, beautiful, full of life, trim, muscles, young, in good shape, physically fit, potent, robust, virile, vigorous, whole, well

MAKE MORE MONEY

Example: I love to make and save money. Money is my friend and is attracted into my life every day. I am financially free, my savings account is growing, and I am in control of my spending. I am surrounded by wealth and abundance. I am a money magnet. Money loves me.

Words: money, rich, affluent, wealthy, abundance, dollars, gold, silver, millionaire, security, luxury, comfort, fortune, valuable, savings account

IMPROVE RELATIONSHIPS

Example: I love my partner, and my partner loves me. Every day our relationship is improving. Our communication improves and opens up more, day by day. Our true feelings come out, and we both listen to them with open hearts and minds.

Words: I love you, heart, caring, passion, warmth, commitment, couple, devotion, fondness, truth, honesty, intimacy, longing, relationship, romantic, embrace, affection, romance, true love, forever, admiration, respect, communication, understanding, support

Master Keywords Technique Creates Highly Focused Power

When engaged in a task with a certain desired outcome, summarize your final goal in a few words and repeat those words in your mind while you are pursuing that outcome.

By doing this, you are basically giving your subconscious mind orders it will instantly follow, telling it the results you want so it will act accordingly. Doing this will also help you focus only on those certain thoughts, or keywords, and block all other thoughts.

Master keywords are commands that bring what the words represent into reality.

For example, when I'm playing a game with a target and I want to hit a bull's-eye, I simply repeat the word *bull's-eye* to myself over and over before I shoot. My likelihood of hitting the bull's-eye increases dramatically when I apply this technique.

When lifting weights, during my reps I repeat the word *strong*.

When I'm tired and I want to sleep, I repeat the words *sleep* and *relax*.

When I'm feeling down or sick, and I want to have more energy and become healthier, I repeat the words *healthy* and *strong*.

When I'm running and I want to run faster, I repeat the words *run faster*.

After much repetition, the words will become part of you. Your thoughts and actions will be aligned with those master keywords.

I had a client named John who loved to go bowling. Even though he was an amateur, he went bowling many times a week. His greatest desire was to become a 200-point bowler.

He wanted to apply the Positive Attraction System to his game, so I taught him the master keywords technique and asked him to visualize himself rolling strikes—the term for knocking down all the pins—and winning games.

John kept a record of his score, and if he rolled a spare, he would erase and rewrite it in the scorecard as a strike. This way, he also erased the spares in his mind and replaced them with strikes.

At home he would relax, close his eyes, and visualize himself rolling strikes and scoring over 200 points. John was very passionate about his game. When he visualized, he was actually living it in his mind and seeing himself rolling strikes, which increased his positive feelings and associated them with his desire. After his visualization sessions, he was very optimistic about obtaining his desire and continued his day with a big smile on his face.

At the bowling alley, every time he went up to bowl, he reminded himself that he was a 200-plus-point bowler and started repeating to himself the word *strike*.

Using the master keywords technique, he quickly increased his bowling average. After a while, just to test what would happen, he stopped using this technique. Not surprisingly, his point average went back down.

Through his highs and lows, John ended up averaging 211 points and was very excited to have surpassed his longtime goal of becoming a 200-point bowler.

It's important to remember that words don't just give or take power from you; they also function as commands that program your subconscious, which is the basis of the master keywords technique. The master keywords technique can be applied to many situations, and it always improves the results of whatever it is you are doing.

Words Give or Remove Power

Words are very powerful and can give or take energy from you.

During a flight to a city where I was going to give a weekend seminar the following day, I was very tired and had a cold. Due to the low cabin pressure, I could feel the sickness affecting the different parts of my body, and I was very attentive to my body's reactions.

I thought I'd take my mind off my illness by reading, so I grabbed the magazine in front of me. The first thing I saw was an article about the poor state of the economy. When I started to read the negative words (even though they were only about the economy), something strange happened, something I had never experienced before. Reading those words actually made me feel more ill, and I started to cough. When I stopped reading and looked out my window instead, my coughing stopped, and I instantly felt better.

The first time this happened, I didn't make the connection. When I started to read the negative words again, my energy level instantly lowered. I felt the negativity affecting my body, and I started to cough continuously again.

This time the negative effects were so strong and I felt so bad that I was only able to read a couple of paragraphs. When I stopped reading, my coughing stopped, I immediately felt better again, and I realized that it was the negative words that were affecting my physical and mental health.

When I realized what was happening, I was stunned. I already knew about the power of positive words and that negative words can push you down and take your positive energy away, but I had never experienced it at this speed or intensity before. It was like turning the switch on and off on my energy level and health. When I fed myself positive words, my health started to improve, and when I fed myself negative words, my symptoms worsened.

If my energy can be depleted by my absorbing negative words, I reasoned, then positive words should do the opposite and raise my energy level and health. So I picked up a book full of positive and uplifting words and images.

I started to feel better: my coughing stopped completely, and throughout the remaining part of the day, my health continued to improve.

After a good night's sleep, the following day and throughout the weekend, I was at 100 percent again. My training seminar went excellently, and I was more careful of what I read and when I read negatively oriented information, if at all.

Forgive and Be Free

Everyone has a set amount of feelings that always totals 100 percent. You have a great amount of control over the ratio of positive to negative feelings. If you do or think of something that makes you feel good and your positive feelings increase by a certain amount, your negative feelings will decrease by the same amount, and vice versa.

You can picture your emotions as a glass filled with clean water (positive emotions) and dirty oil (negative emotions). The best possible option is to fill your container with as much clean, pure, transparent water as possible. An effective way to make room for more positive feelings is by releasing negative emotions that have been locked up inside of you.

When you forgive someone, you remove some of your negative emotions, freeing that space in your container so that positive feelings can fill it up. By forgiving, you are freeing yourself from those negative thoughts and feelings and actually gaining control back from something that at times seemed to be controlling you.

The reality of forgiving someone is pretty interesting. Sometimes the other person involved doesn't know how his or her actions affected you, so he or she probably doesn't understand or feel as bad as you do. This means that you are the one continuing to suffer while the person that hurt you might be living as if nothing happened.

The truth is that the person who actually benefits the most from forgiving is you. You are the one suffering, you are the one who keeps the wound open, you are the one who keeps those negative thoughts constantly in the back of your mind, and you are the one who holds the key to unlocking that pain and setting it free, once and for all.

The benefits of forgiving occur regardless of the severity of the hurt that was inflicted. Even small personal issues result in negative energy and affect you negatively. When you analyze the different parts of your life that may benefit from your forgiving other people, don't overlook the minor ones. Every time you forgive, your positive energy will rise, your spirits will be lifted, and you will feel lighter and happier.

POSITIVE ATTRACTION STEP #4: FEEL

I once bought a car at a dealership. The salesperson told me that the car was in excellent condition, and I took his word for it. Only later did I find out that the car had some major issues. Once I found out the truth, I was infuriated, and my positive energy took a drastic drop. This feeling lasted a few days—until I realized that what had happened was already in the past and could not be undone. All I was doing was taking my positive energy away each time I thought of it. I also realized that I was the only one in this negative state: the salesperson wasn't, my wife wasn't, nor was anybody else.

I forgave him and instantly felt a release of the negative energy. My positive energy filled up that space, and my whole body felt a sigh of relief.

The negative energy brought on by someone else was keeping me from reaching higher levels of well-being, and I was allowing it to.

Notice that forgiving doesn't necessarily have to be done in person. In fact, the other person need not even know you forgave him or her. If you want to tell someone you forgive him, that's fine, but if you don't want to, that is also acceptable.

What matters is that you truly forgive the person in your heart.

My favorite uncle, whom I was very close to during my youth and looked up to as a father, experienced major issues later in life, and his personality gradually turned for the worst. My uncle had negatively affected several people's lives, including mine, though to a much lesser degree. Even though I hadn't been affected as much, I was extremely mad and angry at him because of what he had done to others, so much so that after he once again emotionally wounded a close family member, I decided to end all communication with him.

I didn't try to get in contact with him, and he left me alone. This situation lasted for quite a long time—almost twelve years. I decided that I would only consider forgiving him if he apologized to me. Until that happened, I would live my life as I always had. During this time period, I kept practicing meditation techniques and constantly strengthening my connection with my inner power.

After about eleven years of zero communication with him, one day while I was meditating, I decided to ask my subconscious mind to give me what was best for me at that time. I kept an open mind, asked with an open heart, relaxed, and let go. After a few minutes, something happened that was unexpected and life changing.

I suddenly felt a huge weight lifted off my shoulders, a weight I didn't even know I had, and a thought popped into my mind: "I forgive my uncle."

I didn't know how to react, but a few seconds afterward, a huge smile came to my face. I started to fill up with huge amounts of positive energy, and I felt incredible.

Immediately after I forgave him, my feelings of anger and hatred toward him stopped, and I felt unbiased, with no negativity toward him. Notice that I experienced this transformation having forgiven him on my own, from within, without even needing him to know I had done so.

When you forgive, you release tension and pressure and bring more control into your life. I thought I'd been a very positive and optimistic person all the previous years. Not until I forgave my uncle did I notice that my container had some negative energy in it that wasn't permitting me to be all that I could be.

Forgiving brought immense benefits—benefits I could have enjoyed many years earlier had I simply removed the invisible yet troublesome weight I was carrying.

The shackles were put on my feet by someone else, but the shackles *remained* there because of me. All that time, I had the keys to unlock and the power to remove the chains; all I had to do was forgive.

The past is over. Release the negative hold, liberate yourself, break free, and continue to grow your positive energy so you can live a full and happy life.

Forgive and be free. Your mind, body, and soul will thank you for it.

Apologize and Remove the Extra Baggage

The other side of forgiving is apologizing. When you have self-imposed negative feelings because you've hurt someone, it is important to reduce or remove those feelings so you don't have emotional baggage. The less clutter you have in your emotional life, the more your star will shine, and the happier you will be.

We are human, and sometimes we make mistakes and hurt other people's feelings. Hurtful words said in a fit of anger, actions taken to deliberately hurt others—they all cause painful feelings for the people involved.

Accepting that you were wrong and apologizing to the person who was hurt is very important, for the other person's benefit and your own. When you apologize, you aid in the process of removing negative feelings and energies you set upon yourself and the person affected.

Apologizing makes us humble. When you open up to the person affected, you let your guard down, and that takes courage. You have to accept that the person you are apologizing to may tell you exactly how bad you made him or her feel and even some unpleasant truths about yourself.

Regardless of the consequences, if someone is hurt due to your negative words or actions, do what's best for both of you: apologize and start to eliminate those negative energies.

By apologizing, you are helping the person you hurt to forgive you. This will start the process of removing the negative energy you created so it can be replaced with positive energy.

The Invisible (Yet Very Destructible) Enemy: Fear

Love is what we were born with.
Fear is what we learned here.

—Marianne Williamson

Fear is one of the strongest negative emotions. It is a highly negatively charged thought that is emotionalized and thus impregnated in your subconscious. Fear can affect every nerve, muscle, and cell in your body. It can destroy your positive energy and keep you from seeing how strong and powerful you really are.

As mentioned before, whether you believe something that is real or imaginary, your subconscious mind doesn't know the difference. Your subconscious mind thinks it's real.

Like any negative emotion, fear should be eliminated from your life because it can attract precisely what you fear, bringing your worries into reality. Since fear is an emotion that is attached to a negative thought, it can attract and bring what you fear closer to you.

When fear is embedded in your subconscious, you may start to focus on possible negative outcomes, which can make you behave as if they will come about. Doing so, you may unknowingly mold your fears into reality.

Eliminate fear by replacing negative thoughts with powerful, positive, energy-giving thoughts.

Various Ways to Stop Fear

Fear creates tension in your muscles, especially your shoulders, forehead, eyes, jaw, and hands. As you notice what muscles are tense, begin to loosen them up, and put yourself at ease.

Then start to focus on the reality you are living. Realize that regardless of whether you have fear or confidence, your present situation remains the same. Fear is mostly in your mind.

Sometimes, what we fear is a possible future event or action. For example, you might fear giving a speech, asking your boss for a raise, going to traffic court, and so on.

It has been said that one way to eliminate fear is to do what we fear the most. In other words, confront the fear head on and take control. Of course, there are many different kinds of fears, and not all should be confronted directly.

The good thing about fear is that it is controllable. Recognize that it is based mostly on a thought, and since you have control over what you think and do, you can eliminate most of your fears altogether.

As is done with other negative thoughts, an easy way to stop thinking of what you fear is to replace it with a strong positive thought. A powerful thought can usually be the opposite of what you fear. The following are examples of two common fears and how you can remove them from your thought pattern.

Fear: My Relationship Is Ending

You might be afraid that a good and healthy relationship is ending, and you might make the mistake of talking about your fears with other people and listening to their stories of similar situations that had negative outcomes. You start to believe that your relationship is going to end, regardless of whether there is any concrete reason to believe that it will. You begin to act differently toward your partner on account of your negative thoughts, and your partner reacts differently to you because of this. The chain reaction has begun, and soon you will encounter that which you feared the most.

One way to eliminate this type of fear is to think of and visualize your relationship improving, then communicating with your partner and clearing up any doubts you might have. Be grateful for the healthy relationship you have, maintain confidence that it will continue to be healthy, and learn how to strengthen your relationship in order for it to be long lasting.

Fear: I Will Have an Auto Accident

You are afraid of getting into a car accident. When you are in your car, all you think about is not wanting to crash. Over and over again, you tell yourself that you don't want to crash. Unfortunately, the subconscious doesn't acknowledge the "don't"; what it understands is that you *want* to crash your car. You are actually focusing on getting into an accident instead of focusing on driving safely.

The way to eliminate this fear is to rephrase what you want. Instead of fearing an accident, you should change your thought to one that reflects your faith that you are a safe driver and then focus on that positive thought. Change "I don't want to crash my car" to "I am a good and safe driver." By doing this, you diminish your fear, regain control, and redirect your focus to driving safely.

Why You Shouldn't Socialize with Negative People

Do not sit long with a sad friend. When you go to a garden do you look at the weeds? Spend more time with the roses and jasmines.

—Jalaluddin Rumi

Problematic people will always exist. They try to pass their issues and bad vibes on to you, and you may start to absorb them.

If you spend long periods of time with someone (or a group) with strong negative energies and you don't block the negativity, your positive energies will be reduced.

You might be flowing positively for months or even years, but just by socializing with negative people, you can become engulfed in their flow and exposed to their negative energies. This will put you in a bad mood, make you cranky, and bring about negative thoughts. You will feel as though you have been flowing negatively for months or years, just as they have.

You can try to correct this if the other person's personality is weak and permits a full alignment with your energy. If the negative person has a dominant personality, though, he or she will most likely not align fully with your energy, if at all.

There are ways to prevent other people's negative energies from affecting you. It helps to ignore their negative comments or limit the time you spend with them. Sometimes the best thing to do is avoid them altogether.

We all know and can recognize negative people. During the day when they experience nine positive events and only one bad event, they tend to focus on that one negative event. Even though 90 percent of what happened during their day was good, they make sure that their day seems to have been horrible by focusing on the negative. They also like to make sure that everyone they come in contact with knows how bad their day was. They focus all of their attention and energy on that negative event.

Negative people are not just telling the outside world how negative their lives are, but they are also programming their own subconscious minds to attract more negativity. The subconscious takes that information as a command and will make sure that these negative people bring more of what they are asking for into their lives.

They are effectively canceling out the positive energies and events in their lives and ensuring that their lives are full of problems and negativity.

When they focus on their negative events, they become unable to see opportunities for improvement. They may have something that can benefit their life right in front if them, but since their focus is on the negative, they don't see it.

Their focus on the negative guarantees that their lives don't improve. Instead they repel the good and stay anchored to their position at the bottom of the happiness ladder.

But these negative people, like all of us, can change their thinking patterns. Instead of focusing on the bad, no matter how much of it we have in our lives, we can focus on the good things in our lives.

A positive outlook has the same effects on the subconscious, but with positive outcomes. This means we can effectively cancel out the negative energies and events in our lives and enjoy goodness and happiness.

Negative people exist, and they've always had and will have the option to be positive people.

You can try to guide problematic people in the right direction, motivate them, and show them how to be more positive, but unless they are willing to accept the help and take action to improve their lives, none of this will work. Sometimes helping them works, and sometimes it doesn't. The majority of the time, bettering their lives doesn't depend on us. We can't force people to do anything they don't want to do; it's ultimately up to them.

If they decide to come over to the bright side of the world, fantastic. Let them know you will be there waiting for them. If they choose to remain where they are, that means they still have some personal lessons they need to learn before making that shift.

It's their choice, same as it's your choice to surround yourself with positive people.

A few years ago, a friend of mine had just returned from Europe, where she had lived for about a year. We met her for dinner, accompanied by her sister, my brother, and his wife.

When we arrived at the restaurant, we were all excited to hear of all the great things she'd done and all the wonderful places she'd visited. But mainly we were excited to see her. My friend hadn't seen us in a very long time, and this was the first time she was meeting my brother's wife.

The first words that came out of her mouth were directed to my brother's wife, whom she hadn't been introduced to yet: "Oh my God! What's wrong with you? You don't look so good—are you OK?" She didn't even give us the opportunity to greet her. Her behavior immediately brought down the positive energy level. All the excitement and anticipation about seeing her quickly diminished.

My brother's wife was indeed tired, as she was getting over a cold, but she was smiling and acting normal and looked fine to me. More than a reflection of my brother's wife's appearance, my friend's comment was just evidence of how negative a person she is. In fact, throughout dinner, she kept making negative remarks about her trip and arguing with the waiter.

Though I'd looked forward to enjoying my friend's company for the first time in a long while, all of the positive energy quickly dissipated. Negative people sure know how to attract negative things to themselves and repel the positive, which in this case was the warm and loving welcome home from her supportive friends and family.

Reduce Your Stress Level Right Now

Work, finances, relationships, and other pressures cause stress that can block your inner power from being accessible.

Are the actions and decisions you are making in your life causing you more or less stress than before?

Once in a while, take a step back and analyze your life. Look for opportunities to remove any elements that cause stress.

Think of the issues that create stress in your life, and then rephrase those issues, writing them down as questions:

If you're stressed because your days are too busy and you don't have enough time for yourself, you would rephrase the issue as, "How do I slow down or reduce my daily tasks and still have some time left for myself?"

If you have too many bills to pay, your phone doesn't stop ringing with bill collectors, and you don't have enough money to pay the rent, ask, "How can I reduce expenses and increase my income to stop the bothersome calls and be able to pay all my bills on time?"

If you have a disagreement with your loved one, ask, "How can we come to an understanding that can benefit both of us without hurting each other's feelings?"

If you are ill and your stress level seems overwhelming because of the possible complications that illness might bring about, ask, "How can I most effectively heal my body while at the same time focusing on the good outcomes?"

Rephrasing problems into questions will focus your mind on solving the issues rather than dwelling on them, help clear your mind, and even reduce stress. By applying this process, you will invite your subconscious mind to help you find solutions.

In addition, when you eliminate negative thoughts of problems and replace them with positive questions full of power and hope, you exchange a negative thought pattern for a positive one, and this reduces your level of stress.

Remember that some amount of stress is natural and even good for you, but stress that starts to take a toll on your emotions and health should be lowered and, if possible, eliminated from your life.

When analyzing the causes of your stress, focus on the solutions, not on the actual problems. You should spend your time and energy on resolving the issues instead of lingering on them.

When you are experiencing high levels of stress, keep calm and continue to do your daily routine as usual. Pressure can cause the mind to react differently, possibly causing you to make decisions that block what you want to attract. The less control you have, the more stress you will experience when dealing with situations that you did not expect or prepare for.

Also note that the greater the number of activities you have in your life, the greater amount of stress you might have. By reducing your number of daily activities, you can also reduce your level of stress.

Cut the noise in your life, reduce the stress, and focus on the important things. Make a plan to reduce the amount of stress and number of unnecessary distractions in your life starting today.

Understanding the Death of a Loved One

We were all born, which means that someday we will all pass away. This is normal and natural.

In general, we should strive to get something good out of everything that happens to us. However, this is not necessary when someone close to us passes away. When someone close to us dies, the last thing we want is to dwell on why it happened.

In order to better understand what happens when a loved one passes away, it's essential to accept that our bodies are not only made of physical parts that we can touch and see. More importantly, we are made of intangible parts, parts we can't see even though we all instinctively know they exist.

Our souls may be invisible and intangible, but they are a powerful means of connection with others. Our soul is what we use to create strong bonds with the ones we love. It's our means of truly connecting with one another, hence the term *soul mate*.

Our souls have been with us for a long time and will continue to exist after we are no longer alive. Our souls and their bonds with the ones we love are eternal.

Loved ones may have physically left your life, but their memories and your bond with their souls will live on forever. They will always be with you.

The Toxic Effects of Anger

Anger is a very strong emotion, and in situations that are out of our control, we can get carried away with how we react toward others. Anger can blur our minds and cause us to lose sight of our positive direction, worsening a situation rather than helping to resolve it.

Being angry is like smoking. Like secondhand smoke, anger pollutes and affects everyone in the area in a highly negative way. It can immediately reduce everybody's positive energy and make the whole atmosphere turn tense.

Not surprisingly, the person it affects the most is the angry person. The anger inside is slowly killing the person and contaminating his or her whole environment.

Always try to control your emotions and think rationally before you say something negative or when you are making any important decision. Anger cuts the cord with your inner power and increases the chances of being incorrect when making a decision.

When your mind is not clear to make the correct decision, your negative emotions will make it for you. Even though eliminating your anger might take anywhere from a few minutes to many hours, never make an important decision in an altered emotional state.

Also, don't spread negative energy around. Just because you got angry doesn't mean that everybody you interact with has to be a part of it. Let others' positive energies rub off on you, not the other way around.

Giving Gifts, Compliments, and Help

*Give a little, and receive a lot. Give a lot, and
receive everything that's best for you.*

What you give, you will get back many times over. Whether you give something good or bad, you will get an equivalent or greater amount of the same.

Give a little, and get a lot. Give a lot, and get everything you want. This applies to material and nonmaterial giving.

The number of material and nonmaterial gifts you give should be balanced. You should not only give money and material objects, but also give compliments, give a hand, give thanks, and so on.

Some of the benefits of giving are as follows:
- You feel great.
- The positive energy level of the recipient rises, and he or she will be very grateful for what you did.

- Your star will shine brighter, and you will be attracting more positive things in your life.
- You plant positive seeds that you will harvest in the future. What goes around comes around.

Please note that you should never expect to get anything back from the person to whom you gave. If he or she gives you something back in the future, great. If not, don't worry: everything in this world is repaid eventually.

As we've seen before, if you plant good and healthy seeds, the seeds will grow and give you good and healthy crops. But if you plant bad and unhealthy seeds, troublesome weeds will grow and bring more problems into your life.

What you give is what you get. If you don't give anything, you will get very little if anything in return. If you give good things, you will get good things in return. If you give bad things, you will get bad things in return, guaranteed.

Intangible Giving

When you give someone a compliment, it makes him or her smile and feel good, and in turn it makes you feel good as well.

Offering a simple greeting—a good-morning, good-afternoon, or good-evening, depending on the hour—is a wonderful way to brighten someone's day. Most people are stressed and worried, but a greeting from a stranger momentarily stops them from thinking of their stressful situations and problems. Actually, the fact that somebody cared enough to greet them makes them begin to think about kindness and other positive thoughts.

The following are some examples of intangible giving:
- helping somebody with something he or she needs: offer your help when someone is struggling with a task, picking something up that someone dropped, carrying something that is light for you but heavy for someone else
- paying a compliment: how handsome, beautiful, young, healthy, or happy somebody looks
- greeting people: good morning, good afternoon, good evening, hello, how are you doing?
- giving a quick smile to someone

- holding the door open for somebody

Sometimes the favor may be returned. For example, try saying to your loved one, "Good morning, handsome." He will likely feel very special and warm inside and may return the compliment: "Good morning, beautiful."

As with anything else you give, you should never give a compliment expecting one back. Give for the sake of giving. That said, what usually happens when you give someone a compliment or a gift is that out of the blue, someone else will give you something back.

By giving, you are surrounding yourself with positive energy and attracting more of the same. As the saying goes, the more you give, the more you get.

Tangible Giving

Giving someone a small gift has big effects. The person receiving will feel good even if the gift is small and inexpensive. The saying "It's the thought that counts" is true. The recipient knows you went out of your way to buy a little something for him or her, and that alone will give the person a warm feeling inside.

Giving a gift generates a unique and awesome feeling.

An interesting thing also happens when you give: *your* positive energies grow, and you start to feel really good, even though you are the one *giving* the gift!

What does this mean? Give lots of gifts! They don't have to be expensive; they can literally be anything. You can give whatever you want, even something that didn't cost you a dime.

One Christmas many years ago, my whole family on my mother's side met for the holidays. David, one of my younger brothers, was about ten years old at the time.

As we had done on previous occasions, each family member was randomly assigned to give one gift to someone else. When it was time to start handing the gifts out, one uncle always loved to do the honors. He started by reaching under the Christmas tree, calling out from whom and to whom the gift was, and handing it over to the lucky recipient. The whole process took about two hours.

Just as we were all getting ready to move to another room, my little brother gave us all a big surprise. Nobody knew what he was going to do, so we were all caught off guard.

David got our attention and told us to wait a minute. He rushed out of the room and quickly ran back in, holding a bag in his hand.

Without saying a word, he moved to where our grandparents were sitting and gave each of them a gift. He went around the living room, giving presents to everybody, telling us our name and handing us our gift.

He was creating great excitement and raising the positive energies in the room. At the same time, though, some of us felt a bit awkward because we had given only the one gift that we had to give while this little boy made sure everybody got a gift from him.

After he had personally given each of us a gift, we all started to open them.

What was this special present that nobody had expected? Well, it was a small gift, wrapped with colorful paper and tied with a ribbon. You could plainly see that he had wrapped it himself. When we opened our presents, to our great surprise, what we found inside was a rock! That's right—just a regular, common-looking, out-of-the-backyard rock.

There was absolutely nothing extraordinary about the rock, but nonetheless we all were very touched, amused, and delighted to have received it.

Some of us laughed when we opened up the gift; others were still in disbelief that this little boy had gone out of his way for everyone. But one feeling was universal: he had brightened our day. It was such a nice gesture that I'm still talking and writing about it many years later.

I can still remember that feeling. I felt very special, knowing that someone had gone out of his way for me and others, regardless of what the gift was.

Even giving a thank-you letter, a compliment, or a hand to someone who doesn't expect it will bring a smile to his or her face and make both of your inner stars brighter. The more you help other people to be happy, the happier you will be. What really matters is that you help brighten people's days throughout your life, even if it's by a small amount.

The more you help increase other people's energy levels so their stars shine brighter, the brighter your star will shine.

Start helping to make other people's stars shine brighter, one gift at a time.

Why Being Grateful Is So Powerful

*Be thankful for what you have;
you'll end up having more.*

—Oprah Winfrey

It is very important to be grateful for all the good things in your life. You truly have so much to give thanks for. Even if you think you are currently in a bad situation, the truth is that it could be worse, so be grateful for what you do have.

Being grateful raises your energy level, makes you see the good things in life, and molds you into a more positive person. Even being grateful for the small things in your life will lift your spirits and make your star shine brighter.

When you give thanks for what you have, your positive emotions serve as feedback to your subconscious mind, which stores that information and elevates your positive energy levels.

You start to see and appreciate more of the good things in your life, however small they might be. Also, since you are focusing on the good, the bad will be muted, and you will start to surround yourself with an impenetrable positive force field.

These positive energies will attract more of the good things you want in your life.

 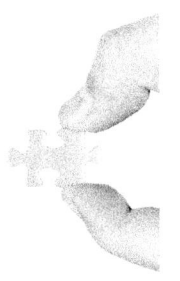

Positive Attraction
Step #5: Visualize

CHAPTER 6

Positive Attraction Step #5
Visualize: Imagine It in Your Mind to Have It in Your Hand

Everything you can imagine is real.

—Pablo Picasso

Visualization is the constructive use of the imagination. Visualizing is similar to seeing with your eyes but without actually using them. When you visualize, you use your mind's eye to see the mental images.

Once you know what you want, start to visualize it. Make it come alive; imagine it to the very last detail. Enjoy it, absorb it, and accept it as yours. You can visualize yourself already being thinner and healthier, wealthier, and happier in your relationships.

Using visualization techniques, you can retrain yourself to be more aligned with what you want. Don't just think it or say it, but actually make it a part of you. Accepting it as yours will make you think and act differently, guiding you toward what you want and attracting it to you faster.

Seeing something with your mind's eye is similar to actually experiencing it because your subconscious mind doesn't know how to distinguish between what your eyes see and what your mind's eye sees.

When you visualize, always visualize the end result: the fulfillment of your desire. You shouldn't focus on how you are going to obtain it; that might change along the way. You have an idea of how to do reach your goal and what direction to start in, but opportunities may come along that will lead you in a different—and often better—direction to obtain your goal.

The doors will open, and you will be shown the way. It might be the way you thought it would be, or it might be a different way. Regardless of how you'll get there, visualize what you want, follow through with action, and soon your desire will come to be.

When applying the Positive Attraction System, repeat this phrase to yourself often: My thoughts and actions are always in harmony with what I desire.

What You See Is What You Will Get

What you see many times will be ingrained in your mind. The more you see it, the more you will believe it. Just as the repetition of words helps mold you into becoming and obtaining what you want, images do as well.

If you have a photograph or image of what you want, look at it often and memorize it so that you can see it with your eyes closed.

It's very useful to surround yourself with images of the things you want since what you most often see gets programmed in your subconscious and will be attracted into your life.

Find images of your major desires, and fill your life with them. Set them as background images on your computer and cell phone. Create a real or virtual vision board, and remove any negative pictures or images that might be bringing you down.

What you *constantly see*, whether it's really happening, depicted in a photo or drawing, on TV, or anywhere else, is what you will attract more of into your life. Like words, images can give or take energy and power from you. If you see negative things, you will be weaker, and your energy will be lowered. If you see positive things, you will have more power and energy.

Always use images that are positive and full of things you want to obtain. You shouldn't use images of activities or outcomes that you want to avoid because your subconscious only absorbs the information (in this case, images) that it is given and will interpret a negative image the same as a positive one.

For example, it's good to look at a picture depicting abundance and wealth, not one depicting lack and poverty. Even if your purpose in displaying an image of poverty was to remind you to avoid that type of situations, your subconscious doesn't know how to distinguish your purpose. It will take all images, positive or negative, as commands and bring them into your reality.

What you see on a regular basis is the information your subconscious will be programmed with and attract into your life. For the most part, you choose what you see, read, and listen to. Try to make all that you are exposed to as positive as possible.

The Benefits of Meditation

People have been using meditation techniques for more than two thousand years. Today millions of people all over the world enjoy meditation, improving their lives in many ways.

Meditation's physiological benefits include the following:
- increased blood flow and slowed heart rate
- strengthened immune system
- decreased stress levels
- facilitated breathing
- slowed aging
- increased energy and strength
- lower cholesterol levels
- easier weight loss

Meditation has psychological benefits as well:
- increased self-confidence
- improved thought control
- improved learning and memory
- increased positive feelings
- increased creativity
- improved ability to understand situations and solve complicated problems

- increased serotonin, leading to mood stabilization, better sleep, and more mental clarity and focus

Meditation also increases the levels of the following mood-enhancing neurochemicals: endorphins (the feel-good hormones), DHEA, and melatonin.

Meditation is free to do, easy to learn, and available to everybody everywhere.

Visualization and Meditation Create a Powerful Combination

Even though meditation is commonly used to clear one's mind and eliminate all thoughts, we will merge some of the process with the Positive Attraction System and focus our thoughts on what we desire.

I like to use the meditation process as a way to quiet the conscious mind in order to access the subconscious mind. As you know, when you access your subconscious mind, you can retrieve information from it as well as program it with any information you'd like.

Since you can only think one thought at a time, meditation gives you the benefit of releasing other thoughts, quieting your mind, and focusing on your breathing. If you then visualize your desires while engaged in the meditation process, your world will begin to transform and improve, inside and out.

The following are some very basic steps to quiet the mind and help you visualize more powerfully. Before you begin, find a location where there are few distractions and your concentration can't be easily broken. This can be in your house early in the morning when you are fresh and ready to start the day, on your lunch break, after work when you are relaxed and at home again, or even at a park, a lake, the beach, or anywhere you feel calm and at peace.

When you are a beginner, reducing the number of distractions is essential so you can focus your thoughts and energy more effectively. With practice, however, you will be able to focus even if there are distractions. It's all mental, and your mind can dominate.

Now sit comfortably in a chair, or sit on the floor with your back straight. You can cross your legs if you'd like, though it is not necessary to do so. What matters is that you are comfortable in whatever position you choose and that

POSITIVE ATTRACTION STEP #5: VISUALIZE

your back is straight. Place your hands on your thighs or wherever they are most relaxed.

After getting into a comfortable position, begin the process by closing your eyes and taking a few deep, slow, and long breaths through your nose. Inhale completely to fill up your lungs, and then exhale slowly to let it all out. After a few long breaths, continue to breathe in a normal and relaxed fashion, and keep focusing on your breathing.

Notice how the life-giving air travels in through your nose, passes through your throat, and fills your lungs. Likewise, also notice how the air flows out. Listen to your breathing, and feel the sensation of the air flowing in and out of your body.

A minute or so after focusing on your breathing, begin to scan your body to identify any parts that are not yet relaxed. Start from the head, and continue downward. Notice if there is any pressure in your forehead, eyes, or jaw, and release the tension. Check your neck, shoulders, and back, and enjoy the sensation of relaxing your tensed muscles.

If you have difficulty slowing your mind and stopping it from wandering, you can count your breaths. Count them from one to ten, and then from ten back to one again. Do this for a few minutes or until you have quieted your mind.

Once your mind and body are relaxed, start to focus, and visualize your desire. Start living it in your mind. The more you see it, touch it, breathe it, taste it, smell it, and emotionalize it, the more powerful the attraction will be, and the faster your desire will become a reality.

See yourself obtaining your goal, and believe that you have already received what you desire. Notice how you feel now that you have obtained your desire, how you act, and what you talk about with others.

Since you have already mentally accepted the desire as yours, your actions will follow and will attract it and manifest it in your life.

With mediation, you bring your conscious mind in contact with your subconscious mind. Having a relaxed body and a quiet mind permits your conscious mind to more effectively communicate its desires to your subconscious, receive answers to important questions, and obtain other useful information.

You can start with just five minutes of meditating a day and gradually work yourself up to ten, fifteen, twenty, or thirty. The more you do it, the better the results will be.

Visualizing your desire with a relaxed and quieted mind, even if it is for only a few minutes a day, will energize your body, your mind, and the desire itself. Visualization gives you the power needed to bring your desire into reality.

Interact with Your Subconscious Mind: Ask, Tell, and Listen

The three most important ways to interact with your subconscious are as follows:

1. Ask. You can ask your subconscious any type of question, such as how to solve a problem, which option you should choose, why something happened, what is needed to improve a situation, and so on.
2. Tell. You can tell your subconscious exactly what it is that you want.
3. Listen. In order to receive an answer, you need to listen.

Ask

When you have a question or doubt, you can consult your subconscious. Keep the question in your mind, and emphasize its importance by focusing on it and repeating it a few times so that it becomes embedded in your subconscious.

After asking your question a few times, relax so that your conscious mind slows down and your subconscious becomes accessible. You will have moments of clarity when you are in tune with your subconscious and will know exactly what the answer to your question is and what to do. Other times it won't be that easy. However, the answer should generally come smoothly and naturally. You shouldn't force or pressure yourself to get an answer; that may only make the process take longer.

If you are not getting the answer you're looking for, it's likely that either you are not asking the right question (i.e., you need to rephrase it more accurately) or you simply need more time to get the right answer.

Note that you can also simply ask for help in any situation you might have. You can ask for assistance in anything you need, and you will receive the help you require. For example, you may ask for help when trying to find the solution for a complicated problem, when trying to improve a relationship, your health, financial situation, and so on.

Asking for help will open up the possibilities for you to receive it more easily.

The answer you get will depend on what and how you ask. The better the question, the better the answer. Sometimes answers will come quickly, and other times, they will take a few days or weeks. As long as you are relaxed and in tune with your subconscious, the answer will come to you at the perfect time.

Rest assured, the answer will always be given.

Tell

You can tell your subconscious exactly what you desire. You can program yourself to do, think, and become whatever you want to be. When you repeat your desires and affirmations, you are telling your subconscious what you want. This is a great way to realign your thoughts to think the way you want to, replace negative thought patterns with positive ones, and program your goals and desires. An effective way to tell your subconscious what you want is by repeating and visualizing it with your eyes closed.

Listen

When you listen to your subconscious, good ideas suddenly pop into your mind. These thoughts may be related to questions you've asked your subconscious, or they may be more random. The best time to listen is when your mind is quiet, your thought process is slow, and you are relaxed and receptive to new information. But good answers to questions and new ideas can come at any time, so be prepared to write them down.

When Is the Best Time to Get Answers and New Ideas?

> *Ask, and it will be given to you; seek, and you will find;
> knock, and the door will be opened to you.*
>
> —Matthew 7:7

At certain times of day, your subconscious is highly receptive and can readily absorb your thoughts and desires. These are the most effective times to ask, tell, and listen:

- when you are in a drowsy state
- when you are taking a bath or shower
- when you are relaxing
- when you are meditating
- when you are engaged in a routine or repetitive task (which lets your mind wander)
- when you are exercising

Even though certain times of day are more powerful, there is no wrong time to focus on your desires. A good time to do it is any time you remember to do so.

The above list includes the best times to tell and program your subconscious with what you want, ask for solutions to any questions or doubts you might have, and, most importantly, listen for answers and ideas. During these times, you will receive good ideas and answers to your questions, and it's important to write them down. You may forget them quickly, and it can be very difficult to remember them afterward.

When You Are Tired and Drowsy

When you are in a drowsy state, your subconscious mind is more accessible. Normally, drowsy states occur when you are either falling asleep or just waking up.

Notice that even though you are drowsy at both of those times, each involves a different amount of energy and receptiveness and a different mood. When you wake up in the morning, you are refreshed. Your conscious mind begins to think, and your energy level starts to rise. When you are falling asleep at night, you are tired. Your conscious mind slows down, and your energy level is low and diminishing.

What you think and feel in a drowsy state will be absorbed by your subconscious more readily than what you think and feel when you are wide awake and active.

Before going to sleep, ask the questions you need answers to, and your subconscious mind will continue to look for solutions even while you sleep. By doing this, you will be feeding your subconscious mind commands that it will carry out in the background. Make sure to limit the amount of times you ask questions before you go to sleep so that you can relax, let go, and sleep peacefully.

For many people, including myself, the subconscious mind is more accessible upon waking. You might find that you stumble and are uncoordinated when you get out of bed. You don't reason correctly, your mind struggles to do simple tasks, and you find it hard to remember things. All of these are signs that your conscious mind is slow, which means that your subconscious is more accessible.

When You Are in the Shower

Water has an extraordinary effect on your physical and mental state. It invigorates while at the same time relaxing and balancing you inside and out. Every day your body comes in contact with large amounts of water when you bathe or shower. Showering rinses your stress and problems away. It renews, relaxes, and realigns your body and mind.

When you are not distracted by the outer world, your senses are soothed and in harmony. You feel the running water on your skin, hear the sound of the drops, see nothing (if your eyes are closed), and smell and taste only steam and water. Even though you are awake, your connection with your subconscious is heightened.

Water enhances the connection to your subconscious mind and the Universal Mind and makes you more receptive:

- Solutions come for doubts and problems that did not appear to have easy answers.

- New and positive ideas suddenly emerge and flow effortlessly toward you.
- Information for the next step to achieving your desires is given, and you can clearly see what direction to take.

The shower is one of the best places to brainstorm and discover solutions to problems. Some of my best ideas come while I'm showering or exercising.

Whenever you feel overwhelmed, stressed out, tired, or are just in doubt and in need of some answers, take a nice long shower to relax, clear your mind, and get solutions to some of your issues, regardless of the time of day.

To make your connection most effective, when you wake up in the morning, try not to think too much, and keep your mind as relaxed as possible. Don't check your e-mail or absorb any information from the outside world before you jump in the shower.

Enjoy your time in the shower, and use it to think about your desires, ask questions you need answers to, and let your mind be free and relaxed. Allow some time for the desires and questions you have to be relayed and absorbed by the subconscious mind.

When you do receive instant ideas, you'll need to make an effort to remember them until you can write them down. After you finish showering, be ready with a pen and paper or your smartphone to record the information you received.

When You Are Exercising

When your conscious mind is busy doing routine or repetitive actions that require minimal amounts of thinking, your subconscious mind has the opportunity to give you important answers and ideas.

I find exercise to be the best way to lower my stress level and at the same time receive answers and good ideas.

When I am concentrating on doing an exercise, my mind temporarily forgets about the stressful situations in my life and lets me mentally relax. In addition, exercise releases endorphins and helps burn excess cortisol (the stress hormone) and adrenaline.

Exercising is a great way to get good ideas and answers to your questions, but it's not so easy to write them down when you are in motion. The information being received is fresh and easily forgettable. If you don't have somewhere to write it down, then dictate it into your mp3 player or cell phone so you can access it later. If you have neither of these available, then repeat the information to yourself every few minutes to make sure you remember it long enough to write it down later.

What Can Block Your Connections

If you aren't getting much or any feedback from your subconscious mind, your conscious mind might be blocked. Your conscious mind can be blocked due to many reasons that include:
- constantly thinking of problems
- being distracted often
- abusing drugs or alcohol or being on certain medications
- calcification of your *pineal gland*
- being under large amounts of stress

Eliminate issues that may be affecting your connection so you can relax and fully connect with your subconscious mind.

Take Advantage of Deep Connections to Your Subconscious

At certain times when you access your subconscious mind (which is ultimately an extension of the Universal Mind), your connection will be more powerful than at other times. When you have a deeper connection than normal, always try to get the most out of it. Even if it's at a time of day when you are very tired and drowsy or you're already lying down and trying to go to sleep, retrieve as much information as possible and write it down.

If information (answers to your questions, good ideas, and so on) is flowing to you easily, continue in that state longer than normal. Keep an open mind, ask questions, visualize desired outcomes, and see what feedback you get from your inner wisdom.

Any type of outside distraction can cause a disconnection from the source feed, activating your conscious mind and cutting off the thought that was smoothly coming to you. Once even a small distraction occurs, your conscious mind may continue to focus on it, and you may forget the information that was being received from your subconscious mind.

Even though information from your subconscious is fresh in your mind and it seems so good that it would be impossible to forget, the truth is that most of the time, you will forget. Forgetting information received from your subconscious mind is normal; it happens to all of us. That's why during or after you finish your connection with your inner wisdom, you should write down all the thoughts and ideas you receive, even those that might not have seemed very important.

Later during the day, or the day after, review and analyze what you wrote down, and make sure that you apply the thoughts that make you feel good.

Information that flows from the Universal Mind through your subconscious mind is priceless. The Universal Mind always knows what is best for you, guides you in the best direction, and can greatly improve your life.

Write the Received Information Down

Receiving information from your subconscious mind is like suddenly being placed in a classroom during a lecture on a new and very difficult subject.

When you attend a real class, you know what time it starts, how long it's going to last, and how difficult the subject is going to be, and you have all the necessary materials and textbooks.

But when you receive information from the subconscious mind and the Universal Mind, you don't know when you are going to receive it (unless you are asking for it), how long the information flow is going to last, or what the content is going to be.

Receiving information from the Universal Mind is like taking a class with a professor who is going to give you the correct answers to the test, but he is only going to tell you them orally. Whether you write them down or risk forgetting them is up to you.

Remember that the information being given is new, and if you don't write it down, you will forget the answers most of the time.

If you find yourself in a situation where you don't have anything available to write the information down on, then keep the information in your mind, repeating it to yourself every few minutes until you are able to write it down.

Always Visualize What You Want, Not What You Don't Want

Whatever you repeatedly see, think, focus on, and visualize is what you will attract.

Let's say you want to lose weight. If you post an image on the refrigerator of a pig or a picture of yourself at your heaviest to try to scare yourself into eating less, you will actually gain weight. Those images will focus your mind on becoming or remaining heavy.

Your life heads in the direction that you focus on, whether that direction is good or bad.

Instead, post a picture of yourself at your trimmest and healthiest. Embedding that image in your subconscious mind will bring about the thoughts and actions needed to become that way again.

Your life is molded by the words, images, and thoughts you focus on.

Associate what you want with something pleasurable that generates positive feelings inside of you.

Positive Attraction
Step #6: Have Faith
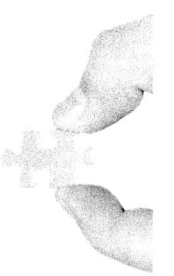

Positive Attraction Step #6
Have Faith: What I Truly Believe I Will Achieve

According to your faith be it done unto you.

—Matthew 9:29

Y ou will receive what you believe in.
In order to achieve anything, you must first believe it's possible. Faith is the invisible force that brings your strong beliefs and desires into reality.

If you ask for what you want correctly and your desire is in tune with what is best for you, you can be 100 percent confident that you will receive it. Don't be tense or desperate while you are waiting; you will get a much better result when you are confident and relaxed.

Figure D-1: When Your Subconscious Mind Doesn't Believe What You Desire

Your Subconscious Mind Does Believe What You Desire

The more you believe and have faith that you will obtain what you desire, the higher the likelihood is that you will.

It helps to repeat the following affirmation to yourself every so often: What I truly believe, I will achieve.

Always Have Positive Expectancy of Achieving Your Desires

It will be done unto you just as you believed it would.

—Matthew 8:13

You should have a positive expectation of obtaining what you desire. You should believe you can attain it even if you don't know *how* you will do so. You get what you expect.

If you say, for example, "I want ten million dollars in my bank account within the next thirty days," will it happen? Probably not.

One of the main reasons is that you don't believe it to be possible. You have to believe in what you desire.

If for whatever reason you don't believe you can achieve your goal, you can program yourself to do so. Engrain the desire in your mind by repeating it and thinking about obtaining it until you convince your subconscious that it can be true.

A client of mine, let's call him Charles, really wanted to get married. He didn't know to whom, nor did he know exactly when, but he knew he was ready and had faith that he would get married soon.

Charles was a very successful businessman with several multimillion-dollar businesses. He had many lady friends whom he would date, yet none fulfilled his requirements for a wife. At the time, making his desire become a reality seemed like a long shot. Using the Positive Attraction System and my coaching, he programmed the thought of getting married in his subconscious, became sure of himself, and was confident that it would happen within the next couple of years.

He became so sure he would be married soon that his subconscious mind was also calm and certain. Whenever he thought about marriage, there was no conflict between his conscious and subconscious minds.

He kept his doors open to opportunities and even gave his ex-girlfriend of many years a chance. They had been out of touch for a long time when out of the blue she started to look for him again.

Since they'd had a few issues before (the reason he stopped seeing her), he really wasn't interested in seeing her again. But she was very nice about it and persistent, and after a few months, he agreed to meet her again—just as a friend, he thought. But when he saw her, he noticed she had changed. The time they'd spent apart not only helped them to know exactly what they wanted in a partner, but it also helped her to mature as an individual.

When we're single, we never know which person will be the best for us, so it's a good idea to leave the door open for opportunities. Charles had already closed the door with his ex-girlfriend, but he also knew that the person he was going to spend the rest of his life with would come into his life and align smoothly with him. So he decided to date her again.

Even though she had been out of his life for a while and he had not considered her initially as a candidate to be his wife, she ended up aligning perfectly with him. She was very interested in building a lasting relationship, and they even talked about having children together.

After a few months of seeing each other again (and testing the waters to reassure himself that the old issues had been overcome), Charles asked her to be his girlfriend. Shortly afterward, he became convinced that she was the one for him, and a few days before Christmas, he surprised her with an engagement ring.

They now live a wonderfully enriched and positive lifestyle full of growth and learning, and they are starting to form a happy and loving family.

When you believe something is possible to attain, you subconsciously begin to act in a different way. Since you have already mentally accepted that desire as a reality, the decisions and actions you make will be congruent with it.

When to Temporarily Divide Desire into Believable Steps

If you don't believe you can achieve your goal, then temporarily modify it or divide it into steps until it's believable.

Your goal can be large and seemingly unattainable, but if you believe that there is even a very small chance for you to attain it, that means it is possible. All you are looking for is the *possibility* for your desire to become a reality.

For example, if you tell yourself, "I have no debts," yet you continue to see the high credit card balances and receive calls from the bill collectors, your subconscious is probably not going to believe it.

Instead you might state it this way: "I am paying off and reducing my debts and will soon be stable and financially free."

The goal is the same—eliminating your debts—but since the phrasing of the second version is smoother and more believable to you, it will be more effective.

You can you still get what you desire even if you find it extremely difficult to attain. When all the steps in the Positive Attraction System are brought together, they create a very strong force that brings you what you desire.

When Not to Believe That You Already Achieved Your Desire

On some occasions your conscious mind will want to believe that your desire is already a reality, but your subconscious won't: the conscious mind thinks one thing, but the subconscious mind doesn't believe it. This situation is known as *cognitive dissonance*. When this happens, you need to believe that your desire is *in the process* of becoming a reality.

For example, I burned my forearm a few years ago, and it was starting to form a scar. I knew that a fresh aloe leaf applied to a wound would make it heal much faster. (Aloe not only heals, but it also rejuvenates.) When I applied the natural aloe, I was also applying my positive thoughts to help heal the wound completely.

I went about visualizing my arm as completely healed, which was easy to do. But trying to act as if it was already healed wasn't so easy. I didn't believe it. I could plainly see that the burn wasn't fully healed. As a result, after several weeks of good progress, the healing stopped.

There was friction between what I consciously thought and what I knew deep down inside was true. In other words, there was conflict between my conscious and subconscious minds, or cognitive dissonance.

Once I began to think about my desire in a new manner, the wound began to heal again.

Instead of thinking that my wound was already healed (which my subconscious didn't believe), I started to think that my wound was healing and improving every day.

I felt better about thinking about it that way because I knew it was true.

I started to say to myself, "My body and skin have the natural power to heal themselves. My cells are healthy, strong, pure, and regenerative. Every day my arm is improving and getting back to its perfect and natural state."

All through the process, I was still visualizing my ultimate desire, which was having a perfectly healed arm. As a result, what could have been a distasteful-looking scar ended up being a very small and hard-to-see blemish.

Doubt and Confidence

A man's doubts and fears are his worst enemies.

—William Wrigley Jr.

Doubt and self-denial are negative thought processes that may prevent you from attaining what you desire.

Doubt overpowers the mind with uncertainty and prevents you from making the right decisions. When you truly think and feel that you can't do something, those are the commands that you are programming yourself to execute.

On the other hand, confidence is created by positive thoughts that are full of energy and give you strength and help guide you in the right direction. Think positively and be confident so you can eliminate doubts and make the right decisions.

Being confident can cause a domino effect: the more confident you are, the better decisions you will make, and the more positive things you will attract.

The Majority of the People at the Top Started at the Bottom

Notice that almost all of the great successes in the world started at the very bottom.

- The majority of highly successful businessmen and businesswomen were regular employees before they ever owned or ran any kind of company.
- The happily married couple you know or have heard of were once single and didn't know as much about having such a loving and happy relationship as they do today.
- The rich and famous actor once only watched movies in the theaters before he ever took an acting class.
- Every teacher was once a student.
- The world-class athlete was once an unknown player in his local school.
- Many multimillionaires started with very little money.
- The perfect mother was once only a daughter.

Just like every professional, in any type of industry, was once an amateur.

Confidence is a key ingredient in obtaining your desires. The more confidence you have, the more control you will have and the happier you will be. Be confident and go forward.

Remember that what you think of and do today, you will be living tomorrow.

Have the confidence to obtain your desires, and start taking action today!

Have Patience

Whenever you want to attract positive things into your life, you obtain better results when you are patient, calm, and confident than when you are tense and desperate.

Apply the Positive Attraction System correctly, and be sure of what you want. If it's the best thing for you at the time, it will come to be. If it isn't, then you will get something that will take you closer to your desire or receive something better than what you asked for. Either way, you will constantly benefit from all your actions, grow as a positive person, and naturally attract more positive things into your life.

Be calm and confident that the results will be positive. Don't get desperate because your desire hasn't become a reality yet. The calmer and more confident you are, the better the results will be. You are in control of your life. Be clear that what you want is best for you, and you will always get a positive result.

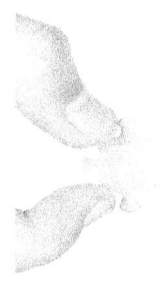 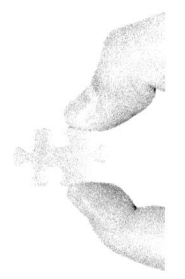

Positive Attraction
Step #7: Receive

Positive Attraction Step #7
Receive Your Desire with Open Arms

*Your desire has come to be;
receive it with open arms.*

Receiving is the last step and doesn't require as much emphasis or explanation as the others. However, its simplicity is no reason to overlook this important step.

It is necessary to be mentally prepared to receive your desire when it comes so that when you are given what you want, you will take it immediately.

Be Mentally Prepared to Receive Important Desires

For very important and possibly life-changing desires, you need to be mentally prepared to receive what you are asking for. Sometimes when your desire is given, you might not be ready. You may disregard it and push it aside.

You have what you want right in front of you, but the lack of preparedness and possible mental blocks can keep you from accepting it.

You have arrived at the last and easiest step of them all, so receive it. Simply say to yourself, "Yes, it was worth it. Yes, I deserve it. Yes, it's mine."

Go ahead and receive it with open arms.

Thoroughly complete the previous Positive Attraction System steps, and you *will* be prepared to receive your desire when it becomes a reality.

Results Are Always in Your Best Interest

If you are a person who thinks and acts positively, the results of your thoughts and actions will always be in your best interest. Rest assured that your life will continue to improve every day, regardless of how much time passes and whether you receive what you desire or not.

The Positive Attraction System is not only designed to attract what you desire. It is also meant to attract what is best for you at that time.

Remember that you can't force your desires to happen. They should happen naturally, at a good pace, and for the right reasons. Some desires might require more time to soak in and for you to align yourself to receive them.

It could take a few minutes or a few years, but the more energy you invest in following the steps correctly, the faster your desires will become reality. Note that if you are positive about what you want, it will always come to you at the perfect time. It will be yours when the time is best for you to receive it.

The more time you dedicate to reaching your desires, the better the results will be and the faster you will attain them.

Why Haven't I Received What I Desire?

Every great man, every successful man, no matter what the field of endeavor, has known the magic that lies in these words: every adversity has the seed of an equivalent or greater benefit.

—W. Clement Stone

Simply being alive means that hope exists. Positive opportunities will always be available to you, now and in the future, so keep your eyes open, and be ready to take action. Every day is a new and fresh beginning full of unlimited possibilities.

Just because obtaining your desire didn't work the first time doesn't mean it won't work the second or third. Keep analyzing why you have not reached your desire yet, learn from your attempts, and realign your life in the best direction. Your inner power is there to help you reach all of your desires. It always wants the best for you, no matter what situation you might find yourself in.

There are four main reasons you didn't get what you desired:
1. More time is needed for it to manifest. (Keep moving forward and looking for opportunities.)
2. You don't believe it's possible. (Program yourself to believe it or divide the desire into more believable steps.)
3. Your approach is incorrect. (Try other approaches.)
4. It is not the best desire for you. If this is the case, then new paths will open up towards a destination that will give you something better in its place. (Analyze your current situation; perhaps you've already received something better.)

If your desires are positive and you do the steps correctly, your inner power will guide you and always bring what is best for you at that time.

Remember that you are like a magnet full of living energy. Through your thoughts and actions, you attract similar events and people into your life.

In the realm of living energy, like attracts like. Positive attracts positive; negative attracts negative.

What you think, feel, and do attracts similar things to you.

If you improve from within, your outside will improve as well.

Once you improve, your actions will align with your positive way of thinking, which in turn will bring you the positive results you desire.

Focused Energy Equals Success

All the main steps that repeat in the Positive Attraction System require energy: thinking, taking action, adding feelings, having faith, and practicing visualization. This energy should always be aligned and focused on your desires.

Figure E-1: Unfocused Energy

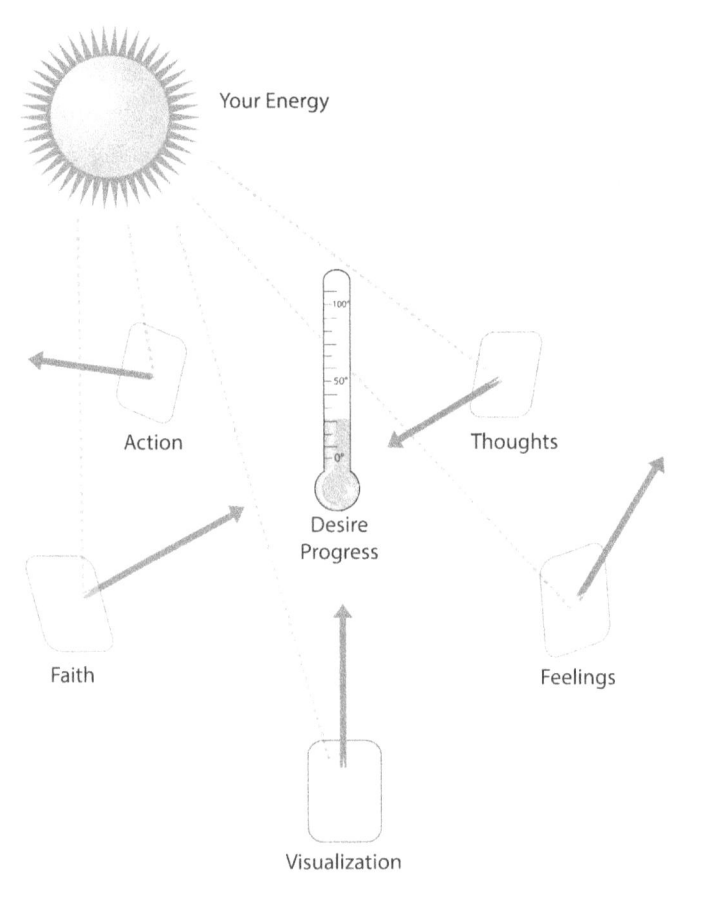

If you focus only a small amount of energy on your desire, you may wait a long while for it to be fulfilled, if it ever is.

All of the ingredients should be aligned and pointing in the right direction. The more these ingredients are aligned, the better the results will be.

Figure E-2: Focused Energy

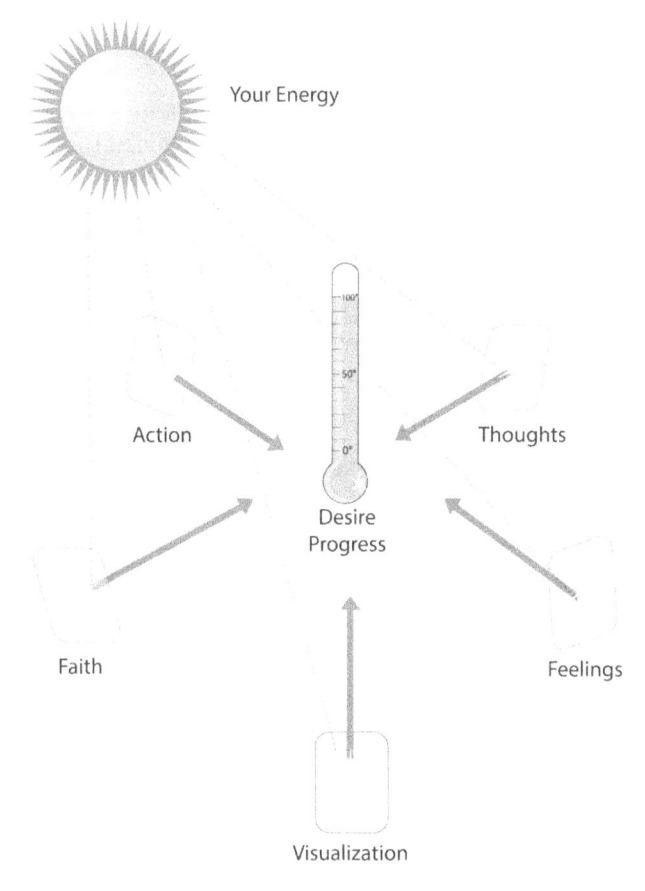

Focusing all your energy toward what you desire brings great results.

When all the ingredients are directed toward the same goal, the energy will be so great that your desire will come to be.

If You Didn't Receive What You Desired, You Will Get Something Better in Its Place

We sometimes think we know what we want and what is best for us. Yet there are times when the best thing for us is something we didn't expect.

Your inner power always knows what is best for you. If there is something better than what you asked for, you will receive that instead. Or you might receive something that will put you on track to reach your original desire, which means that more learning, time, and action are required.

When all the steps for the Positive Attraction System are done correctly and the timing is right, there are two main possible outcomes: (1) you get what you asked for or (2) you get something better.

We are human, which means we are constantly learning. We still do not know everything there is to know. But our inner power always knows what is best for us.

If you apply the Positive Attraction System correctly and let your inner power guide you, you will achieve more than you have ever imagined. Go with your inner power's natural, positive flow. It is always working in your best interest.

Rest assured that if you ask for something well meaning and beneficial, the result—even if it's not exactly what you expected—will always improve your life.

Consistency Pays Off

The more consistent you are with practicing the Positive Attraction System, the better the results will be. If you dedicate a short amount of time every so often, the results will be slow and sporadic. If you dedicate a few weeks of constant practice, you will get the ball rolling. If you make a constant effort over a few months and incorporate the system into your way of life, you will attract not just your initial desires, but all the other benefits of being a more positive person. Good things will constantly come to you because positive thoughts and actions always produce positive results.

Enjoy Today and Every Day

You are alive here and now. You will soon reach your goals and receive all your desires; in the meantime, be grateful and give thanks for what you have today.

It's good to have many desires and goals, but don't wait until you receive them to be happy. One thing is guaranteed: time passes. Make sure you live your life to the fullest, always.

Make the most of your life today and every day. Even if your life is not ideal to you, make the most of it. Be as happy as you can be, and enjoy your life. If you don't, the best years of your life will pass you by before you know it.

Today you are as young as you will ever be again. Enjoy it.

Even if you think the best years of your life have passed you by already, you are alive right now and reading this book, so start enjoying your life, and stop thinking of what could have been. The past doesn't equal the future. The past is not changeable, but your present and your future *are*. You are in control and can mold them into whatever you want them to be.

Know and accept that you and your surroundings may change, and that is normal and natural. Everything is in a constant state of change, so appreciate what you have in this moment.

Enjoy today and every day.

Positive Attraction in Your Life

You are a very powerful person and already have all the essential tools needed to obtain all that you desire. You naturally have an incredible amount of inner power that attracts what you want, guides you, and always knows what's best for you.

Align your thoughts with your actions to attract everything you want into your life.

When you apply the steps of the Positive Attraction System, no matter what the result might be, it will make you grow in every aspect of your life, guiding you in the best direction possible.

Always remember, the amount you receive is equivalent to the amount of effort you put in. The more time and effort you invest in doing the Positive Attraction System correctly, the better the results will be.

Take action today, and start living the life you have always wanted to live. Be happy, be strong, and be in control of your life's direction.

The more positive and happy you are, the more positive and happy the people around you will be, and the more you will attract your desires into your life.

Positive Attraction is powerful and contagious. Share the good energy!

A Personal Word

My Dear Friend,

You already possess everything you need to reach all your desires. Bring Positive Attraction into your life today, and start attracting all the positive things you desire. Begin to move forward with the first steps—even if it's just by writing down your desires—and start bringing them into your life right now.

Always remember these three phrases:

- Whatever is best for me, my positive thoughts and actions will make it be.
- My thoughts and actions are always in harmony with what I desire.
- Whatever I truly believe, I will achieve.

May all that is best for you come smoothly and continuously, now and forever. Wishing you a life full of love, health, and wealth.

Yours truly,

Walter Marin

About the Author

Walter Marin is the founder of the Positive Attraction System and is a top expert in helping people enrich their lives.

Marin has taught and implemented the Positive Attraction System throughout his life, with extraordinary results.

An internationally renowned author, coach, and speaker, Marin is also a successful million-dollar business owner and entrepreneur with various university degrees, including a Bachelor of Arts in International Business and a Master of Science in Finance from San Diego State University.

Marin is currently a full-time author and enjoys helping people through his coaching practice and seminars.

To learn more about Walter Marin please visit:

www.PositiveAttractionAcademy.com

Like: fb.com/WallyMarin | Follow: @WallyMarin

www.ingramcontent.com/pod-product-compliance
Lightning Source LLC
Chambersburg PA
CBHW071916290426
44110CB00013B/1376